AFTER THE RAPTURE

The Truth for the
Christian Church
And the
Terminal Generation

John H. Boyd, Doctor of Ministry

PRESS

TABLE OF CONTENTS

INTRODUCTION vii
FOREWARD ix
CHAPTERS
  1. WHAT DOES CHRISTIAN MEAN? 17
  2. WHAT IS THE RAPTURE? 27
  3. THE AGE OF GRACE 34
  4. NO SECOND CHANCE 40
  5. MYSTERIES OF THE RAPTURE 48
  6. SATAN'S PLANS 55
  7. MILLENNIAL GROUPS 64
  8. SAVED THROUGH FAITH 77
  9. FIRST SCENARIO 85
10. THE HOLY SPIRIT'S ROLE ON EARTH 91
11. STORY I: THE UNCHURCHED 99
12. RELIGION AFTER THE RAPTURE 112
13. THE REIGN OF THE ANTICHRIST 119
14. THE APOSTLE'S PROOF 124
15. A MASTER DECEIVER 130
16. TRIBULATION SALVATION? 136
17. THE CHURCH OF SOCIAL REFORM 143

18. THE UNREPENTANT CHURCH 149
19. STORY II: THE LOST CHURCH MEMBER...............156
20. GOOD PEOPLE? 170
21. A HOLY SPIRIT-LESS WORLD 178
22. A CURRENT DECEPTION 186
23. COUNTERFEIT CARING 193
24. RECOGNIZING THE TRUE CHURCH.....................199
25. HOW MANY WILL BE RAPTURED?.......................203
26. AMERICA REJECTS THE GOSPEL........................208
27. STORY III: THE RAPTURE 221
28. THE JUDGMENT..234
29. THE DEAD IN CHRIST..................................241
30. ISRAEL AFTER THE RAPTURE 255
31. SIGNS OF THE TIMES: 263
   A. WARS AND RUMORS OF WARS........................263
   B. PESTILENCE AND DISASTERS 265
   C. JUST LIKE THE DAYS OF NOAH........................267
   D. LIKE SODOM AND GOMORRAH 270
   E. THE MEDIA-SHAPED CULTURE 275
32. CONCLUSIONS 279
33. I AM A PRE-TRIBBER — REVELATION 19 287

INTRODUCTION

I was a teenager when I first learned about the rapture. I may have actually heard the word 'rapture' earlier during my childhood, but I never thought about its meaning until my teen years. Of course my level of comprehension was that of a typical adolescent. I heard about it and thought about it, but I assumed that it would not happen during my lifetime.

Although I had heard about the rapture, like most teens I never spoke about it. It was just one of those 'church words,' and not used in everyday conversation. I should also mention that there were many other things I knew very little about, and yet somehow felt competent to discuss. But not the rapture! Maybe somewhere way down deep I was frightened by the mysteries associated with the serious side of religion. Hey! I was a kid! Who knew that one day I would actually be living out that which I believed?

During my hectic teen years (1961-67) there was plenty of talk about nuclear war and such in America. The thought of being suddenly blown away by the Russians really kept my buddies and me on the edge! In the midst of growing paranoia, who needed the idea of being suddenly snatched away at the rapture? Even though the two concepts were miles apart, they both embraced the notion that for us everything could change instantly and forever!

This line of reflection has led me to the conclusion that most church members do not relish the idea of the rapture precisely for that reason. Maybe our psyches have built-in defense mechanisms against thoughts that include every-thing we have ever known being instantly changed forever! Or maybe the whole concept is simply too wild and weird to embrace on the level of actually talking about it publicly!

Whatever the reasons may be, it is obvious that most Christian churches today either outright reject the idea of the rapture, or they downplay it in order to avoid disruptive and divisive controversies. Whatever their reasons may be for not acknowledging the significance of the rapture, this book is designed to bring to light one of the most important doctrines of the true Church of Jesus Christ. Jesus will appear to His believers before His return to earth. He is going to amass together in the sky those believers who He has resurrected from the dead and those believers who are alive. The bodies of those in both groups will be glorified in order to accomplish such an event. This is the Rapture of the Church of Jesus Christ. I believe it will happen very, very soon.

FOREWORD

What is the rapture? Although the word 'rapture' does not appear in Scripture, we can find the concept and the description of the event. In First Thessalonians 4: 17 we find the Greek word *harpazo,* which is translated *take (by force)* or *catch (away, up).* The Latin word used is *rapiemur,* meaning *snatched up; carried off.* The word in both the King James Version and the American Standard Version is translated *caught up.* It is understood by believers in the context of a future event during which the bodies of Christians will be instantly changed and taken away (*raptured from*) the earth to be with Jesus forever.

On that occasion, all of the people who have accepted Jesus of Nazareth as their crucified Savior and risen Lord and God will suddenly disappear from the view of those who have not. Instantly their bodies will be supernaturally altered in order to exist in the realm of heaven. Prior to this instantaneous metamorphosis, the bodies all of the Christians who have previously expired throughout the ages up to that moment will be likewise changed and resurrected. Both groups will join the Lord in what Paul described as a realm above the earth.

Christians refer to this event as the Rapture of the Church of Jesus Christ.

This book is designed to answer many of the questions that arise upon reading the preceding thesis paragraphs. Possible questions that will be addressed include the following:

1. Who are the Christians?
2. Why is the event called the Rapture of the Church?
3. What is the importance of the rapture?
4. How will the physical bodies of Christians be changed?
5. What will become of the glorified bodies?
6. What will happen to people who are not Christians?

Hopefully the reader will also find the answers to many other questions that should logically arise during the course of careful clarification.

It is important at the outset to state my belief that the Rapture of the Church of Jesus Christ is an undeniable and inevitable event. The rapture is prophesied in Scripture by such reliable authorities as Jesus, the Apostle John, and the Apostle Paul. Therefore, it shall certainly take place as prophesied and promised. Exactly when it will occur is of no real significance to true believers. This is attested to by the fact that an absolute date and time has not been revealed in Scripture.

However, Jesus has outlined for His believers an unmistakable chronology of events that will precede the rapture. He has also indicated many clearly identifiable world circumstances to reveal the timetable during which His reappearing will occur. The absolute fact of its certain occurrence is all that matters. That Jesus said it would happen at an unexpected time should cause all believers to live in a state of constant preparedness. Of course, if a person is a Christian, he or she will quite joyfully and supernaturally maintain a lifestyle that attests to a distinguishing level of readiness.

The mere mention of people disappearing and reappearing during this era sends most minds racing to the fantastic scenes in science fiction movies and television programs. It is commonplace in this era of cinematic special effects to see people teleported from one place or time to another. People are often depicted as being *beamed up* into an alien space craft, whisked off to another galaxy, and returned several years later looking the same as they did at the time of their abduction! Baby boomers and senior adults have grown up with "Star Trek" and other futuristic science fiction programs.

I'm sure that if one of today's teenagers were to witness the dematerialization of someone, their first conclusion would lean toward alien abduction! Think about it! There has been no other time in all of history when an entire generation of humans would be more susceptible to a reasonable explanation for the sudden, mysterious disappearance of numbers of people. Given both the reliability of the promises of Jesus and the susceptibility factor of this generation for accepting an incredible cover-up theory, I submit that this is most likely the generation during which the rapture of the church will take place.

Likewise, anyone suggesting that the rapture of the church has already occurred must not be given credibility. There are simply too many other indications that ours will be the generation during which the Lord reappears in the clouds. These indications will be addressed in this work. After weighing in on the reliability of these factors, I consider it my responsibility to share with this terminal generation some thoughts as to the coming event known as the Rapture of the Church.

It is true that during the past few decades a number of books, television specials, and movies have made various attempts to address the occurrence of the rapture. Many of those publications and productions promote the false hope that those who miss Jesus at the rapture will receive other chances to believe in Him during the aftermath. It is, after all, one of the goals of feel-good religions, as well as box office-hopeful movies to have a happy ending for as many of their members or viewing audiences as possible. Let's call it effective marketing!

I believe that such marketing hype and the sensationalistic appeal of Hollywood movies have rendered most of these former projects invalid. No doubt their success formula certainly must appeal to the masses. To someone who does not understand the Gospel, it must seem right that non-believing Gentiles who witness the rapture will certainly line up by the millions to belatedly accept the Lordship of Jesus Christ. After all, anyone, upon seeing that the Bible was actually true concerning the rapture of the church, would suddenly be moved by shock and awe to believe in Jesus!

It is my belief that those who promote the concept that Gentiles who have rejected Jesus during the Age of Grace will receive another chance for redemption after the rapture are laboring under satanic deception. It smacks of giving believers a false impression that they need not press people with the truth of the Gospel. They are less fruitful because of the comfortable idea that, if someone doesn't accept Jesus before the rapture, they will certainly accept His lordship after witnessing the rapture!

To reject the Gospel before the rapture is to call Jesus a liar. Such a rejection of the Gospel is, therefore, a form of blasphemy! It is blasphemy of the Holy Spirit. Likewise, attempts to frighten people into accepting Jesus in order to participate in the rapture must be viewed as a type of anti-evangelism. For example, people who join a church fellowship simply to escape being left behind will most likely not take part in the rapture. While a healthy reverence toward the wrath of God is necessary when considering sinful disobedience, a healthy understanding about the rapture points out that salvation is much more than just fire insurance! The rapture is also a reward from God that will spare His true believers from the final seven years of tribulation terror that will follow the event.

Seen primarily as a means of escape, the rapture loses its intended and essential value. People will be included in the rapture only because they have chosen to accept Jesus Christ as their Lord and Savior apart from the cowardly concept of escapism. True believers have a relationship with God that is based on both their love for Jesus and their love for all other people; not just their love for their own skins!

A true Christian loves God whether there will be a rapture or not! Understanding that the God of the universe loves us and paid a great personal price for our salvation is the motivating force that draws us to Him. A true and abiding love for God is something that people can neither be frightened into nor forced into by external pressures. People are loved into a relationship with God. His Holy Spirit shows the truth found in His Word that reveals God's pure and extreme love presented in the incarnation, loving actions, crucifixion, and resurrection of Jesus Christ. Jesus is God's atoning blood-sacrifice for the sins of all people. The simple truth is that people truly love God because He first truly loved them. The good news is that God still truly loves all people!

This book should not be confused with others that attempt to frighten people into accepting Jesus as their Savior. It is merely an attempt to share my beliefs with other believers concerning what will take place on earth following the Rapture of the Church. By explaining the utter hopelessness of those who are left behind, it is my hope that believers will be inspired to redouble their efforts in sharing the love of God in Christ with as many people as they possibly can before the rapture occurs.

This book, therefore, is written for believers in the spirit of trust, enlightenment, and encouragement. I trust that Christians know their duty as outlined by the Great Commission. Since many believers never consider the concept of the rapture, I pray that this enlightenment will serve to awaken in them many new creative ministry ideas. I encourage all Christians to rise to new levels of commitment in the joyful acceptance of Christ's challenge to tell the world about His love for all people!

The facts concerning the rapture of the church are neither secretive nor guarded. Anyone who possesses reading and comprehension skills can find plenty of information about the rapture of the church in the Word of God. However, only those who possess the Holy Spirit will regard the event as being significant. Both Jesus and Paul spoke plainly enough concerning its reality and pre-eminence. Though the rapture is an important doctrine of the church, it should never be used as a plan of approach when sharing the Gospel with people who have not received Jesus as Savior and Lord. The nature of the rapture serves as non-essential information when shared with either an individual who does not believe in Jesus or with a new convert. Non-believers will only be mystified by such a discussion, and new believers will possibly be tempted to put off their own discipleship training in light of the coming rapture.

New converts to Christianity do not necessarily have to be schooled in their responsibility to tell others about God's great love. If you have ever been around new converts, you know that their whole demeanor reflects the joy of their salvation. They simply can't help sharing with others what the Lord Jesus has done in their lives! People are neither saved nor are they discipled because of information about the rapture. Biblically, they are saved and then discipled. Ultimately, all of those who are becoming disciples of Jesus will be raptured because they are consciously preparing themselves as eternal servants of the Lord!

CHAPTER ONE

WHAT DOES CHRISTIAN MEAN?

B efore going into any discussion about the rapture of Christians, we should first establish what makes a person a Christian. Within the context of this book it would be simple enough to say that a Christian is a person who will take part in the rapture of the Church. A Christian would also be classified as a member of the Christian Church. However, noticing the great excess of groups that call themselves Christian churches, one must then ask, "Which Christian church?" This is a question that drives apostate groups into an emotional frenzy! The simple answer would then be, "The Church of Jesus Christ!" Only those who make up the Church of Jesus Christ are Christians in the Biblical context. And that's where the discussion of what constitutes being a Christian should begin.

A Christian is many things. He or she is a person who believes that Jesus Christ is the Son of God who was birthed by a virgin named Mary in Bethlehem. A Christian believes that the power of the Holy Spirit of God brought about the pregnancy supernaturally. Therefore, according to Scripture, the child that was born is Jesus, the holy Son of God and God the Son. This same Jesus was reared in Nazareth by Mary and her husband, Joseph. According to an overwhelming number of fulfilled Bible prophesies only Jesus of Nazareth could possibly be the Messiah of God. The term "*messiah*" describes the individual that God promised to Adam and Eve, who would come to save their progeny from their sins. The Messiah would be the remedy for the broken relationship between God and every member of mankind.

A Christian believes that Jesus is the Messiah, the Son of the Living God and, therefore, God the Son. That principle was authenticated by Jesus in His response to Peter's confession. Jesus asked Peter, "Who do you say that I am?" Peter answered the soul-searching question by stating, "You are the Christ, the Son of the Living God!" Upon hearing Peter's divine revelation, Jesus revealed His plan for all who would believe the same truth. He proclaimed that His Church would be those people who *based their lives on* the truthful and foundational thesis that He is the Christ, the Son of the Living God! That makes Jesus the Messiah, God the Son, and the object of worship by His Church.

Jesus further explained that the rock-solid truth of that belief was so powerfully penetrating that even the gates of hell could not prevail against the evangelistic thrust of His Church. Christians, therefore, are those who fear neither death, hell, nor the grave based upon their faith in Jesus as the Messiah, their eternal deliverer, and the restorer of their souls. Christians know that they will never die! The word *retreat* does not exist in their vocabulary. The highest form of this kind of courage was seen during the early centuries after Jesus' ascension when believers were tortured and murdered for their allegiance to Him. They were publicly vivisected, burned alive, or fed to lions for their refusal to obey those who demanded that they denounce Jesus and affirm Caesar as their lord!

The reader is admonished to take note of the new paradigm described by the phrase *based their lives on* used in a preceding paragraph. Jesus said that not everyone who cries, "Lord, Lord!" will enter the kingdom of heaven. Even the demons believe that Jesus is the Christ of God! They believe in His name, but they tremble rather than obey Him as Lord. Christians are those people who believe in the name of Jesus *and serve Him* by obeying His laws and commandments to the point of total sacrifice. For Christians Jesus IS their life!

There is another warning found in the words of Jesus that all Christians must heed. He stated that there would come a time when people would be worshipping many false christs. These other christs are worshipped by highly religious cults, denominations, and other organizations that promote a politically correct, non-spiritual version of Jesus. Many of these groups are even headed by deranged megalomaniacs who call themselves Christ. Such a time exists today.

In recent decades there have emerged cult leaders who have somehow managed to beguile sincere followers into believing that they were modern day messiahs. They range from guys named Jim and David to sci-fi types who are awaiting the arrival of a mother ship to beam them aboard and take them away from it all!

The most flagrant yet religiously and politically correct example is found in the Church of Jesus Christ of Latter Day Saints. This cult dishonestly claims validity as a mainstream Christian denomination. Though its adherents use the Book of Mormon for its anti-Christian doctrines, they also use the King James Version of the Bible as a socially recognizable credential. The use of the KJB is for enticing the marginally versed, nominally-committed, non-believer members away from the many and various other mainstream Christian denominations.

The major truth that separates the Mormons from true Christianity is quite simple for anyone with an average IQ. The Mormons believe that Jesus is the spirit-brother of Lucifer, whom we know as Satan. Although from a purely mythological perspective this makes for a great storyline, the Bible truth is sacrificed for emotional sensationalism. The Holy Scriptures identify Jesus as God the Son, the second person of the Trinity. Satan is identified as a fallen angel once named Lucifer, who was generated by God. The true relationship of Jesus to Lucifer is that of the Creator to the created.

The Apostle John greatly simplifies the process of determining the true Christian from the anti-Christian. According to John, true Christians are those who say that Jesus is God and obey His commandment to love one another. The proof of our Christianity is seen in how we faithfully display our love both for Jesus, who is God, and for others. Though we may say that we love God, we must love others as we love ourselves, or we simply do not qualify as a Christian! While Christians must indeed love others, the fine line that separates true Christians from those posing as Christians is ultimately seen in *how* they love others.

Social Gospel posers believe that caring for the human needs of the less fortunate is the highest expression of Christian love. Generally, unless needy individuals are converted by the Word of God, they have a tendency to become totally dependent on those organizations and churches that love the good press they receive for their highly humanitarian efforts. Unfortunately for the needy, those organizations and churches don't care enough about them to share with them the life-changing Gospel, complete with follow-up discipleship programs. On the other hand, Christians understand that the most loving act one can render is to tell people how they can inherit eternal life. They promote God's forgiveness for sins. They proclaim eternal life in heaven with God who created everything and wants to have a personal, eternal relationship with all people through His Son, Jesus Christ!

A Christian knows that God loves every person He ever created and does not desire that any should perish in hell. Therefore, a Christian knows that all people are potential believers. As a person who has accepted Jesus as Savior and Lord, a Christian has also accepted the Lord's commission to share the Good News with everyone he or she may encounter for the rest of his or her earthly life until the rapture of the Church of Jesus Christ.

Christ is the Greek word for the Hebrew word, *Meshia,* which in English is translated *Messiah.* The Messiah as seen in Scripture is God's promised deliverer from the penalty of sin. Messiah is that one-of-a-kind individual whom God would send to restore the spiritual relationship between Himself and man that was broken by Adam's disobedience. In order to serve as the atoner for the sins of all of mankind the Messiah had to be both completely God and completely man. Only God would and could provide such a remarkable way of mending the broken relationship between Himself and His creation.

Adam and Eve, the first humans, had broken that relationship in the Garden of Eden when they disobeyed God. When tempted by Satan, Eve ate the fruit that God had forbidden her and Adam to eat on penalty of death. She was beguiled by Satan's intentionally misdirective suggestion that eating the fruit would make her more like God. Believing Satan's tempting suggestion, Eve ate the fruit. When she did not instantly die from eating the fruit, she offered it to Adam, and he also ate. Adam's sin of disobedience sorrowfully brought the curse of sin and separation from God upon all future generations of man. The Apostle Paul wrote that sin entered the world because of Adam.

Sin is more than simple disobedience. According to Jesus, sin is the fruit or manifestation of a desire to do evil. People initiate sin against God in their minds. All sin is either directly or indirectly against God. Yes, to sin against one's brother is to sin against God, who commanded that we love our brothers. Do mental sins carry the same judgment as physical sins? Jesus said that to look upon a woman with lust in one's heart is the same as committing adultery with her.

The universal truth is that as a man thinks, so he is or does! Therefore, the same is true for any evil or harmful treatment we might mentally visit upon those whom we dislike. The

Bible says that sin comes from the heart of man. Therefore, all humans (including Jesus) are born with the capability to commit sin. Likewise, all humans are born with the capability of choosing not to sin! Jesus is the only man born of woman who has always chosen not to sin. For His obedience God has made Jesus Lord of all.

Because of their sin, God cast Adam and Eve out of the paradise known as Eden. What died that day was the face to face relationship man once had with his Creator. Mankind was barred from ever seeing God's face while dwelling on the earth. Sin created a gulf of spiritual and physical separation between man and his Maker. However, God mercifully made a promise that He would one day provide a way of relational restoration. Jesus, the Messiah, is that way!

When a person accepts Jesus as God's offer of restored relationship, the Holy Spirit of God takes up residence in the heart of that person. God is once more with man! From that moment forward the Holy Spirit serves as a guide for the individual in areas of truth. He comforts the individual with the understanding both of God's loving presence while on earth and of eternal life with God later in heaven. He convicts the person's heart of sin, convinces the believer to confess and repent of sin, and seals the eternal relationship between the believer and God, the adoptive Father.

Approximately four thousand years after Adam's dismissal from Eden, Jesus was born of the Virgin Mary and the Holy Spirit of God. His purpose was to restore God's intimate and personal relationship with mankind. Jesus is the promised Messiah, the Christ of God, and God's method of restoration.

Because He never sinned, His perfectly innocent blood can serve to cover the sins of the entire world. However, it is only a potential covering until men have accepted God's gracious offer of forgiveness. All who accept that loving offer of forgiveness, recognizing that it was Jesus who paid the price for their sins, and respond by making Jesus the Lord of their lives become Christians. Only the blood of a sinless man who also was God in the flesh could have provided what sinful mankind needed for salvation.

Before the coming of Messiah, the sins of the Israelites were systematically atoned for by the blood of animals through various sacrificial, ceremonial rites. A designated high priest would ceremonially cut the throat of a bull or a ram and direct the flow of its blood onto an approved temple altar. The carcass of the animal would then be roasted. By these and other ritual acts the sins of the people would be ceremonially cleansed until the next scheduled time of altar sacrifices. All of these events were tied into the Israelite temple worship of God.

Sacrificial blood offerings were the result of the universal law of God, which stated that only by the shedding of blood could sin be atoned for. Without the shedding of blood there is no remission of sin. Without God's work of atonement, the wages of sin is death. In this case that meant the death of the innocent animals that must be sacrificed in the place of human sinners. God, because of His mercy and love toward mankind, accepted the blood sacrifice of the animals as a covering for the sins of men.

At the prescribed times for the ceremonial sacrifices, Hebrew families brought their unblemished animals to the priests. The priests then slaughtered the animals and smeared their blood on the sacrificial altars. This ritual served to satisfy the requirement of blood as a sacrifice for the sins of those families who offered up the animals. The process was prescribed by God to temporarily restore the sinners' relationship with Him. Thousands of years and millions of animal sacrifices later, God would provide His only begotten Son, Jesus, the only innocent and perfect God/man, as the final blood sacrifice for all people of all times and places.

Since the crucifixion, burial, and resurrection of Jesus, the ceremonial rite of animal sacrifice has been non-effectual. The sins of mankind have been mercifully covered by the precious blood of Jesus, the Lamb of God. Any butchering of animals today in order to re-establish a right relationship with God is both spiritually pointless and ignorantly paganistic. People must forget about all of their substitutional methods of relating to God. Jesus said that He is the only way to a right relationship with the Father! Interestingly enough, even though most Jews still reject Jesus as the Messiah, they have discontinued the practice of blood sacrifice as the atonement for their sins!

Jesus, the Messiah of God, has provided mankind with the one and only genuine path toward eternal peace with God. The Apostle Paul wrote that Jesus once and for all time provided the blood that would cover the sins of all people. On His blood-stained cross we see the fulfillment of God's law that required innocent blood as payment for sin. In His substitutional death we also see the fulfillment of the words of God's prophets and His promise of a Messiah who would serve as the way back to a restored relationship with the Father.

After reading the descriptions of and predictions about Jesus that qualify Him as the Messiah, let's look at that word *Christ* again as it is applied to His believers. As Christ, the Messiah, Jesus saw His responsibility to give His life as a ransom for many. How can we appropriate the name of Christ and be called Christians? Jesus said, "As the Father has sent me, I am also sending you." He further paralleled our mission with His by calling us the "Light of the world," a title that was His. A Christian, therefore, is one who carries out the responsibilities of Jesus, the Christ, in bringing to all of mankind the Good News of God's love for all people. A Christian is a person who has believed upon Jesus as both the Messiah of God and God the Son. A Christian believes that with His blood and by His death Jesus paid the price for the sins of all of mankind. A Christian is a person who appropriates this truth in the form of unquestioning belief in and personal, lifelong allegiance and obedience to the Son of God as Savior and Lord forever. Are you a Christian?

If you are not a Christian, and you are reading this book strictly on the basis of personal interest in various areas of religious thought, you may find some fascination. I hope you will find the love of God that can make you His child forever. If you consider yourself a Christian I pray that this treatment of the Rapture of the Church will cause you to redouble your evangelistic efforts in view of the immediacy of the event.

CHAPTER TWO

WHAT IS THE RAPTURE?

The word *rapture* carries at least three definitions in the dictionary:

1. Overwhelming happiness: a euphoric transcendent state in which someone is overwhelmed by happiness or delight and unaware of anything else;
2. Christian mystical transportation: a mystical experience of being transported into the spiritual realm, sometimes applied to the second appearing of Jesus Christ when true believers are expected to rise up to join Him in heaven;
3. Raptures: a state of great happiness or enthusiasm about something, or words and gestures that express this state such as *went into raptures about the meal they had.*

Though the word "rapture" is not in the English Bible, it has been used so widely that one of the definitions of "rapture" in

Webster's Third New International Dictionary Unabridged is: "Christ's raising up of His true church and its members to a realm above the earth where the whole company will enjoy celestial bliss with its Lord." The modern dictionary also refers to the late 16th century French usage either directly from or through Medieval Latin *rapture*, meaning *seizure*, from the Latin *raptus*. From this word we also have derived the English word *rapt.*

The English word *rapt* has the connotation of having been taken over by a greater force such as delight. For example, when we are enthralled by a rapturous symphonic movement, we say that our senses have been captured or overwhelmed to the point of near delirium. We have emotionally lost touch with our surroundings! We are carried away by the intense rush of musical sensation brought about by the combined harmonies and rhythms of various artistically played musical instruments! We are lost in a moment of musical madness! We're really gone, man!

The word *rapture* is used by Christians to describe their sudden departure from the earth when Jesus extracts His church out of this world to join Him in the air. At that moment, an incredible change will occur for all believers, living and deceased. Regardless of where they are or what they are doing, all true followers of Jesus will be physically taken up to meet with him in a realm above the earth. Currently Christians enjoy a bonding spiritual relationship with Jesus through the indwelling Holy Spirit of God.

Jesus explained the rapture and the situations surrounding this event when He said that two would be working together side by side and one would be taken. He also said that two would be sleeping together in bed and one would be taken. Of course, theologians who do not look for the eminent reappearing of the Lord can find several optional meanings of the words of Jesus.

The most common misinterpretation applies these words to events that occurred in 70 AD at the destruction of Jerusalem. Such theologians are too quick to dismiss the possibility that Jesus, being God, was referring to at least two events that were separated by two millennia! It is dangerous to file the context of the words of Jesus away as being merely historical in essence. We must always remember that Jesus is not only a pure priest; He is also a perfect prophet.

The Apostle Paul was much more descriptive and pointed with his understanding from the Holy Spirit concerning the Rapture of the Church. He wrote to the Church at Thessalonica that at the sound of the Archangel and the blast of a trumpet the Christians who were in their graves would be raised with glorified bodies unto eternal life. In succession, the Christians who were alive would be clothed with glorified bodies in an instant as they were being caught up in the air with Jesus and the newly resurrected others.

This *catching up in the air* is what we refer to as the rapture. Christians would not be able to be caught up in the rapture in their earthly bodies. That's why Paul says that our bodies must be changed from what is corruptible into that which is incorruptible. Our new bodies will be glorified, and so will be like the glorified body of Jesus! We know this because Paul wrote that he did not know exactly what the new bodies would be like, however, he concluded that our bodies would be like the resurrected body of Jesus. He wrote, "We do not know as yet what we shall appear as, but we know that when He comes, we shall be like Him."

Christians whose physical bodies have expired will be resurrected as the first event during the rapture. We must understand that for them time, as we know it, ended the moment they expired. From their perspective, their physical resurrection from the dead occurred simultaneously at the moment of their death. For them no time will have passed. At the point of their earthly death they were seamlessly raptured into the presence of The Lord and all believers past, present, and future!

We can believe this to be true because Jesus said that those who believe in Him, though they were dead, yet shall they live. And those who live and believe in Him shall never die! This He said as a matter of perspective concerning those who knew that Lazarus had been dead for four days. He then resurrected Lazarus from the tomb. We can only imagine how Lazarus must have reacted upon this first resurrection. As a believer in Jesus, he didn't even know he had been pronounced dead and entombed. He only knew that he blinked, heard the voice of Jesus calling his name, and there he was. Lying in a tomb wrapped in burial clothes! And not a moment had gone by since he blinked!

So it shall seem to all those who die in the Lord. Believers who have expired are referred to as the dead in Christ. They have never been dead to Jesus; only to us. Death has been defeated for all believers by the resurrection power of Jesus.

They will appear to have risen first because those who are still alive, but have instantly been given a new heavenly body, will rise to meet them in the air with Jesus. No wonder the Word of God says, "Blessed are the dead in Christ!"

The Apostle Paul wrote about the seeming death of believers. Under the inspiration of the Holy Spirit, Paul said that when we are absent from the flesh (our old bodies) we are present with Jesus. As humans we sometimes forget that from God's perspective time has a different meaning. We simply cannot wrap our minds around a timeless perspective! Try this on for size. When people die, what happens to them? Do they lapse into what some have called 'soul sleep?' When Jesus saw the young girl who was supposedly dead, He said that she was merely asleep. Though the people mocked His assessment, He was speaking to their limited, time-bound perspective. To them, she was dead. To Jesus, she was asleep. What was her actual status? We know that Jesus hadn't ascended yet, so the girl's death was simply part of God's plan to show the power of the Son of Man over death while He was on the earth.

If Jesus had already ascended and the girl had been a believer in Him, she would have experienced the resurrection of the saints at the rapture, even though to the rest of the world the event would be over two thousand years in the future! If she had reached the age of accountability when children know that they are sinners in need of a Savior, and had not trusted in Jesus for the forgiveness of sins, she would have simultaneously risen to her judgment and eternal condemnation. Her resurrection would not take place at the time of the rapture. Only Christians are involved in the rapture.

There are many differing viewpoints as to the theological use of the term 'rapture.' Much will be assumed on the part of this author. The first assumption is that those who have died while trusting in Jesus Christ as their Lord and God, the evidence of which was seen in their obedience to His commands, will rise from their graves with new bodies and meet the Lord in the air. The bodies of those who are alive at that time and meet the same believers' criteria will be instantly transformed physically and will meet the others with Jesus in the air. This is the perspective given by the Apostle Paul in a letter to the Thessalonian Church.

Another assumption of the author is that of the pre-eminence of the event. That the rapture will occur is a given due to the words of Jesus and the writings of Peter, John, Luke, and Paul. Therefore, it is not the purpose of this work to sell anyone on the idea of the rapture. This book is also not an extended dissertation on the rapture. The subject matter deals with a very different approach to the rapture. What will occur on earth following the rapture is the focus of this treatment. Should the reader be uninformed as to the concept of the rapture of the Church, I have included a brief summary of the highlights surrounding the event.

As the time of the rapture approaches, it must be understood that with each passing moment its occurrence draws nearer. As with all planned events, the final phase will involve an acceleration of events and activities that will increase exponentially as the moments count down. Jesus referred to this rapid acceleration of fulfilled end-time Bible prophesies. He gave a list of circumstances that signify the beginning of the final days before He reappears to rapture His believers out of earth's realm. At the exact appointed time following the fulfillment of each prophesy, Jesus will bring the Age of Grace to an end.

CHAPTER THREE

THE AGE OF GRACE

The Age of Grace is defined as the era wherein the Gospel will be offered to Gentiles. During this period, Jews and Gentiles who receive Jesus as their Lord and God will be given the *power to be called the sons of God* (John 1:12). As sons of God they will become *joint heirs with Jesus.* As joint heirs they will receive from God a place of eternal significance in the Kingdom Age to come.

The Age of Grace began when Jesus was born. Some might argue that the Age of Grace began after Jesus was resurrected or after He sent the Holy Spirit at Pentecost. I believe that during His life on earth Jesus, full of grace and truth, displayed for all people the incomparable grace of God. In all that Jesus said and did He graciously showed the way for men to find peace with God by His merciful and gracious forgiveness of their sins. God sent His only Son to die in the place of all sinners. When people believe this and place their trust in Jesus as God's gracious offer of love and forgiveness, their sins are cleansed by the atoning blood of Jesus, the sacrificial Lamb of God. By His grace we are saved through faith (Ephesians 2:8)!

Following His resurrection and before His ascension to the right hand of the Father, Jesus promised His disciples that He would send the Holy Spirit to aid and comfort them (John 16:7-15). The indwelling of God's Holy Spirit serves as the seal of our salvation. He equips and empowers us to tell the world about God's love for all mankind. The Spirit directs us into all truth by reminding us of everything that Jesus has commanded in the Word of God.

The Holy Spirit was necessary to the establishment of the early Christian Church. He worked in the life of the Apostle Paul, who was not with Jesus during His earthly ministry. Paul (formerly Saul of Tarsus) was confronted by Jesus on the road to Damascus some time after Jesus' ascension. Before the life-changing encounter, Saul enjoyed his position of Pharisee and the religious ruler in charge of persecuting Christians. He sought them out and arrested them, bringing them in chains to stand trial before other religious rulers for judgment, which sometimes lead to their execution.

After his conversion, Paul was used by the Holy Spirit in the establishment of Christian churches in many countries. Under the influence of the Holy Spirit of God, he penned much of our New Testament as he wrote letters of instruction and encouragement to the churches he had founded. This same Spirit of God is available to all who become believers during this special dispensation of time called the Age of Grace.

The Spirit's functions have not changed. He convicts of sin, undergirds with truth, and seals believers as the redeemed of God for all eternity. An important difference between the Apostles and believers of today is that the Apostles actually saw and experienced the works of Jesus. They heard not only His words of instruction, but also His tutorial explanations. After the Lord's ascension, God's Spirit reminded them of every word and deed of their Lord and Master.

Since Jesus has ascended to the Father, people must now read or hear the Word of God before the Spirit can commend it to their hearts. Post ascension believers must exercise a much greater faith in order to see their Savior and God eventually. We must trust in the authenticity and validity of the Word of God as found in the available Scriptures, and then depend upon the leadership of the Holy Spirit. Unless people hear the Word of God and trust the leadership of the Holy Spirit, they cannot be saved from the destruction that will fall on mankind after the rapture.

Imagine a world without the presence of the Holy Spirit in the lives of believers! Hatred, violence, and lawlessness will be the order of the day. There will remain no standard of truth. The godly moral compass will have departed. There will be no believers on the earth! Completely sinful men will govern without mercy or grace. The mighty will take full advantage of the weak. For a period of time the hearts of men will be ruled by their selfish egos with no thought or care for the rights of others. Godly grace will not be applied in any of life's circumstances. The status quo will truly become *every man for himself!*

For a time following the rapture many churches will continue holding their religious services. Some of these churches will operate under their own doctrines of grace. Today there are many denominations and cults who refute the idea of the rapture. Needless to say, they will not participate in it. Their church organizations will continue in full operation for a while. Soon enough, however, the evil men who will assume all governmental control will see such organizations as subversive to their overall plan of total domination.

Let's examine what it might be like in a church that continues to meet following the rapture. Just imagine a service in a church building where the congregation pointlessly muddles through ceremonial rituals without any noticeable movement of the Holy Spirit. Picture the lifeless sermons, uninspired singing, and the absence of all challenges to evangelize! One might think that those left behind would be filled with remorse having missed the rapture! Shouldn't someone passionately attempt to convince the congregation of their need to repent and believe in the real Jesus? Of course they should! And that's precisely what should be happening today!

Surely the reader has at some time attended a church service that closely resembles the one just described! Such a congregation does not thrive on the movement of the Holy Spirit. The people are motivated to attend those churches by such ideals as social interaction, family or peer-pressure, and cultic oppression. Many attendees have no idea why they attend their churches! Now you know what is missing from those church services. The Holy Spirit of God is missing! The rapture will have no effect on those congregations.

Without the inspiration of the Holy Spirit, people do not possess the ability to understand the Scriptures. Likewise, they are not able to experience the Holy Spirit convicting them of their sins. Neither is there any supernatural, convicting power to convince them of their need to repent. Some might be instinctively aware that something is amiss, but without the truth of God that is supplied by the Holy Spirit, they can not even know what is missing. Although this scenario is the status quo in many churches today, after the rapture it will be the order of the day in all churches everywhere! The recurring nightmare will become reality at the end of the Age of Grace following the rapture.

How can I say that the Holy Spirit will be removed at the rapture? In the second chapter of Second Thessalonians, concerning the end of the Age of Grace, Paul stresses that at a certain point the Lord will remove the *restraining force.* The restraining force that keeps sin in check during the Age of Grace is none other than the Holy Spirit of God. It is not righteous men who hold the kingdom plan of God on course, but God's own Spirit within His believers. Let's concede that sin does exist, and that it does destroy the unity of the brethren.

However, during the Age of Grace the gates of hell cannot prevail against the Church of Jesus Christ! Because of the Lord's presence in the lives of believers, the ability of Satan to completely dominate the earth is held in check by the Spirit of God. It is only during the Age of Grace that men can respond to the Spirit of God and receive God's gracious offer of sonship and eternal life through Jesus Christ. The focal question for the current generation should be, "What will happen on earth at the end of this Age when the Holy Spirit is removed?"

It is at the point of the rapture that the Holy Spirit will exit the earth. He is now on earth functioning as the motivating force of Christianity. Jesus said to His disciples in Acts 1:8 that they would receive power when the Holy Spirit came upon them. After that they would be His witnesses in Jerusalem, in Judea, in Samaria, and to the ends of the earth. Therefore, from within His true believers, God's Spirit is leading them in all areas of truth. He is empowering them to go *to the ends of the earth* with the message of His offer of a personal and eternal relationship with Him through His Son, Jesus.

God furnishes Christians with the *Essence of God* deep within, thus providing them with faith to be obedient to their unseen Father. It must be understood that when the rapture takes believers out of this realm, the Holy Spirit exits with them. Paul writes that it is only after this event that *the man of lawlessness* will seize control of all the earth (2 Thessalonians 2:7-8). He will only be able to do so because the *restraining force* of the Holy Spirit will have been removed at the rapture.

CHAPTER FOUR

NO SECOND CHANCE

Now to the primary thrust of this book. It is my desire to inform the reader of the truth of God concerning the era that will follow the end of the Age of Grace. Many theologians have given utmost care and numerous hours to the pursuit of aiding the Christian community in their understanding of apocalyptic times and concepts. Many have written books and screen plays depicting scenarios that might follow the Rapture of the Church. For decades there has been reliance upon various *left behind* scenarios, which have served to offer hope for those who might have missed the Rapture of the Church. Pastors have even put together video studies and packets for those church members who were not *changed in the twinkling of an eye* into beings that can inhabit heaven.

It is my belief, encased in my humble opinion, that the possibility of receiving a second chance to believe in Jesus after the rapture and during the subsequent seven years of tribulation is non-existent for Gentiles. Furthermore, it is also my firm conviction that extending such a hope is in direct conflict with the very words of Jesus. Additionally, I believe that such an offer is borne out of either Biblical illiteracy or satanic deception.

Let us consider the absurdity of *second chance* ideology. There is no doubt that during this Age of Grace many have found that Jesus is *the God of the second chance,* and not only of a second chance, but also a third and a fourth, etc. Peter asked the Lord how many times he should forgive others. He supposed that Jesus would consider him gracious for offering to forgive someone up to seven times. Jesus responded with a number 70 times greater. It is suggested that the Lord was putting no limit on the number of times we must forgive others.

During this Age of Grace forgiveness is indeed unlimited! The Apostle John wrote (John 1:14) that Jesus was 'full of grace and truth.' He is the Chief Agent of Forgiveness! Many individuals I have encountered have despairingly said, "I've sinned way too much for the Lord to forgive me," or "I've fallen away from the church" or, "I've strayed too far from the path to come back," I remind them that while they still have breath and the Lord hasn't reappeared, they can be forgiven! Then I jokingly say, "You're still alive, and I'm still here, so the Lord hasn't called us yet!"

That is the nature of this era called the Age of Grace. During this age it will never be too late to call on the name of the Lord and be saved. During this age, *today* is the day of salvation! God freely offers the forgiveness of sins and the indwelling of His Holy Spirit as long as the Age of Grace continues. However, the rapture signifies the end of this Age, whereupon the world enters a time of great tribulation and wrathful judgment.

At the rapture those who have accepted God's offer of eternal life will rise to meet Jesus in the heavenly realm. Those who remain on the earth will begin a fearful time of tribulation and judgment during which there will be no mercy. As ominous as that sounds, it must be noted that there will have been over two thousand years of grace and mercy during which every person on the planet could have called on the name of Jesus for salvation. Furthermore, all who showed no mercy in their own judgments of their fellow man during this era will receive no mercy during their judgment by God.

Those who declined God's gracious offering of eternal life in Jesus will begin to live out the unimaginable conse- quences of their foolish decisions. There will be no mercy shown them because Jesus and the Holy Spirit of God will be absent from the realm of earth. No one on earth will be able to experience the inward conviction of sin. This is true because the Holy Spirit, whose purpose it is to convict men of their sins, will have exited the earth realm. There will remain no Spirit-revealed truth to convince men of God's grace because the Spirit of Truth will have withdrawn from the earth for the appointed time of judgment.

A revealing answer for Bible students is found in the question, "What did Jesus say would happen to those (the Pharisees) who saw His days on earth and rejected Him as the Son of God?" (Matthew 23:13-38) The connecting question is just as poignant. Did not Jesus say that He would be 'with' his believers always, even to the end of the age? (Matthew

28:20) The truth is that Jesus, the light of salvation, has been seen on the earth in His believers for over two millennia. The world has observed the love of God and the testimony of His Word through the personal witness of all true believers. If the Jews of old did not receive a second chance, then why should those who rejected Jesus during the Age of Grace receive another chance?

The truth is that Israel's utter rejection of Jesus as the promised Messiah of God brought about serious consequences for the Jews. Those consequences include the destruction of the temple in 70 A.D. and the global dispersion of the Jews. The temple in Jerusalem was the representation to the Jews of the presence of God among them. It was literally His house! The destruction of the temple was a graphic illustration whereby God withdrew His presence from those who had rejected His Son. The severity of their sin is indicated by the fact that the Jews lost Jerusalem as their home and Israel as their nation for nearly two thousand years!

You may ask, "How does the idea of a second chance conflict with the words of Jesus?" Jesus gave many parables concerning the expediency of receiving God's Salvation. The most declarative statement involved the truth that the Spirit of God will not always strive with men. Plainly said, there will come a time when men will not have access to the revelation of God that the Holy Spirit now supplies. This time will arrive when the Spirit is removed from the earth realm. There is absolutely no way for the carnal mind of man to understand the Word of God apart from the Holy Spirit's enablement.

Only the Holy Spirit can enlighten and convince us of spiritual truths. He is our Guide sent by Jesus from God.

Another unsettling question involves local church members. "What about pretender Christians?" Pretender Christians are church members and non-members who claim to be believers in Jesus, but have no personal relationship with Him. Suppose the rapture occurs on a Saturday night. On Sunday morning, as the pretenders sit bewildered in their reserved places on their own church pews wondering where some of the other saints are, will they begin pleading for a second chance? Or, according to their standard practice, will they just start criticizing and condemning those who are absent? How long will they sit ignorant of what has happened?

Pretender Christians of today have yet to be tested by an event as conclusive and revealing as the rapture. They never even place themselves in the position of professing or defending their faith. After the rapture, there will be no doubt as to who the true believers were. Will the pretenders who are left behind even understand that they have missed it because they are not true believers? How will they ever be convicted of their sin without the convicting power of the Holy Spirit? They never hearkened to Him before, and now He isn't present to be hearkened to! If the Spirit of Truth is not available to reveal the truth about what has happened, how will they ever know the truth?

Carefully consider the seemingly logical reasoning that usually follows such a question. Some well-intending soul will no doubt ask, "Wouldn't anyone who has ever attended church and heard about the rapture surely remember and cry

44

out to God for mercy and forgiveness?" Most sane people will initially give pause to consider what seems to be an obvious and believable reaction. In light of all the 'rapture hype' within the religious community during the 1970's and continuing to the present day, this would be an obvious conclusion. It is unlikely that someone attending church since the 1970's in the South could have missed hearing about the rapture.

Those who have heard of the rapture have subdivided themselves into several categories as to the credibility of such a phenomenon. Some, upon hearing about the sudden disappearance of all Christians at the rapture, voluntarily sink into profound denial of such an incredible notion. Even though they profess to be Christians, they are content to dismiss the concept. Even after hearing their pastor declare the certainty of the rapture, they, nonetheless, disregard the idea in the same fashion by which they regularly disregard other truths that call for Biblical faith. Even upon reading the Scriptures that provide detailed prophesies concerning the event, they are content to rationalize it away. Some migrate to more comfortable atmospheres within church groups that provide alternate explanations for 'rapture' Scriptures.

A large number of Christians, upon hearing all of the *rapture hype*, quickly jump on the bandwagon and began tooting their horns. The awakening of the spirit of the rapture created a groundswell movement within many churches. Soon there were numerous books, both pro and con, to help guide the religious community into various pockets of ideology. On one extreme there were those who were selling off their worldly belongings in preparation of the event. On the other extreme many were emphatically searching for ways to discredit any suggestion that Christ was coming soon to rapture his church. Those in the middle ground began thinking about the end of the age for the first time in their lives.

During thirty three years of ministry in Southern Baptist churches I have seen many fascinating things within the Christian community. Way up there among the most fascinating has been my observation of church members taking from the Scriptures only those teachings and doctrines that conform to their personal dispositions. If a particular teaching calls for a radical adjustment in their life styles, they tend to ignore, overlook, shun, or otherwise down right deny both the validity of the teaching and the application of it to their lives. This personal editing of the Scriptures for convenience sake is practiced on a wider scale than anyone would dare admit, hence the number of "Christian" denominations. The dismissal of the Scriptures that verify the rapture as a real and soon-coming event falls in this category of Scripture denial.

It is, therefore, quite possible that many church members who will be left behind after the rapture, will not have a clue as to what has happened. The prize for their life-long labor of Scriptural denial will be the clueless look on their faces as they survey their hopefully depleted congregations. It may be emotional denial of such colossal magnitude that they dare not allow their memories to go back to that time when someone preached about the Rapture of the Church.

When the rapture does occur, just imagine how stupid one would have to feel after rejecting such a highly publicized and well rehearsed concept! For clarification it should be noted that church members will not be sitting in their pews after the rapture simply because they did not believe in the rapture. Anyone who is not among those who are raptured will have been left behind because he or she did not truly accept Jesus as Savior and God. However, it is difficult for this author to believe that anyone who has accepted Jesus as Savior and God would not also joyfully accept the truth that He spoke concerning the rapture. In Matthew 24:39-41 Jesus speaks plainly of a scenario depicting believers disappearing and non-believers being left behind.

CHAPTER FIVE

MYSTERIES OF THE RAPTURE

Perhaps one of the greatest hindrances to the acceptance of the concept of the rapture is all of the mystery surrounding the event. Most distressing to many is the idea that no one on earth can know the day or the hour that the rapture will occur. No doubt this missing ingredient keeps the faithless from investing their lives in such a concept. Jesus referred to the event as coming like a thief in the night. He added that though we cannot know when the thief is coming, we can prepare for the eventuality by remaining in a constant state of readiness. After all, if we could know the day and the hour of His coming, there would be no need to operate on the basis of our faith. People could live ungodly lives right up to the hour and then confess, repent, and accept God's grace. That is a perfect example of presuming upon God's grace. That's why God won't allow it! Our faith in His Word is what pleases God! In other words, if we trust in the truth that the rapture is coming, we can rest in His Word and live accordingly.

It is not really so difficult to believe that many church members will miss the rapture. Jesus is quoted as having said that on the Day of Judgment many who thought they were bound for heaven will say to Him, "Lord! Lord, open to us" (Matthew 25:11-12). His deflating response will simply be that He does not know them. These will be people who have had the best of all chances to hear and accept the truth of God. How could they have missed the truth when they had a wonderfully convenient chance to hear it every Sunday? Bibles are plenteous in America. There's a church on nearly every corner. There are several 24/7 Religious Broadcasting Networks on both radio and television. America has enjoyed centuries of religious freedom. Yet, for many people the term *rapture* is about as meaningless as the term *born again*. Will they suddenly wake up to the truth after the rapture occurs? Of course not!

There is a very disturbing element found in the many fictional books and screenplays depicting the post-rapture experience of those left behind. The stories are based on some Biblical truth, but are accurate only up to a point. It is the fictional conjecturing that carries potentially grave danger for Biblically illiterate readers and viewers. The stories begin with the rapture. Believers disappear and those left behind are befuddled and depressed.

The usual departure from Biblical accuracy expresses itself in the form of a Christian underground network. The network is set up by people who were either related to believers or closely associated with believers. These individuals now believe in Jesus due to the fact of the rapture.

Once the network is established, more and more lost church members or friends and family members of believers begin to understand what has happened. They finally comprehend what their (now missing) Christian friends had so passionately witnessed to them about. As their *eyes* are opened to the truth, they fall on their knees and accept the Lordship of Jesus! In other words, they are now able to trust *by sight* the Bible truths that their Christian friends or family members were able to accept *by faith*.

There is a very important question that must be considered. If Christians are saved by grace *through faith*, how are those who rejected the grace of God saved *without faith?* The very serious issue I have with fictional literature that depicts thousands coming to Christ after the Holy Spirit has been removed is not really that difficult to understand. There has been given only one way that people must be saved. We are saved by trusting in the Word of God. We are saved by faith. We cannot depend on our sight and then call it faith. Faith comes by hearing the Word of God. We walk by faith and not by sight.

Think about the disciple Thomas (John 20:24-29). Thomas would not believe until he saw the wounds on the resurrected Jesus. Regardless of the eyewitness accounts of his faithful fellow followers, Thomas was ready to spend the rest of his life doubting the resurrection of Jesus. We must remember that Jesus had told the disciples on several occasions that He, the Son of Man, must suffer and die and be resurrected on the third day according to the Scriptures. Thomas not only had the prophets but the very Word of God Incarnate as a personal resource. Was it the depths of sorrow and acute disappointment in the death of Jesus that stifled his ability to trust the words of the other disciples? Does he get a pass for his doubtfulness based on the mental anguish of losing a dear friend and beloved teacher? Why do you suppose Thomas chose not to believe?

Jesus used the unbelief of Thomas as a teaching tool for all generations. He told Thomas that the greater blessing would be possessed by those who would choose to believe without seeing! Isn't that, after all, the ultimate definition of faith? According to that definition of faith, if you have to see Christ to believe in Him, you'll never believe in Him, because on earth you'll never be able to see Him! Someone who says that *seeing is believing* will never see the kingdom of God. We can't have faith if we must see to believe!

But as rational beings how can we believe in something we cannot see? There can be no doubt that we definitely need assistance in this all important matter of believing without seeing. Jesus did not leave His believers groping in the darkness for truth and meaning. Jesus placed within His disciples and all who would come to trust in Him the light of spiritual reason to provide all the vision needed to become *the light of the world.* After the ascension of God Incarnate, God the Spirit was sent as an ongoing spiritual revelation to abide within all those who would believe without seeing. When Jesus commissioned His followers to take the Gospel message to the world, He promised and then delivered at Pentecost the Holy Spirit of God, who supplied them with the power to accomplish His commands. The Spirit of God reveals God's truth to and through those who receive Him. Like Jesus had said to Nicodemus (John 3:3), when we are born again by the Spirit of God, we are enabled by the Holy Spirit to see the kingdom of God with spiritual eyes.

Those who reject Jesus also reject the guidance of the Holy Spirit. These are defined as those who are lost in the darkness, refusing to walk in the light. They have become the children of darkness. They have chosen to follow the Prince of Darkness. Out of desperate denial they will even debate the existence of their Prince. Many take on the appearance of holiness by joining local churches, but they deny the power of holiness by refusing to obey Christ's commands. They may have read the Bible, taught Sunday School, and even delivered many sermons from behind pulpits. They may be good old boys who would give you the shirts off of their backs! They may tithe their income and support many worthy causes around the world. They may have the industrial sized, authorized King James Bible strategically placed in a prominent place in their homes. The simple truth is that if people do not choose to place their faith in the unseen but highly publicized Son of God as their graciously given gift from the Father for the forgiveness of their sins unto eternal life, they have forfeited their souls to the darkness of eternal hell.

Imagine for a moment the sneakiest of all approaches to manipulate well-intending people into doing something that they would never do. If you could ever convince people that what they are doing is actually a good thing, you can pull it off. The first step is to get people to place a higher value on their human reasoning and feelings than on the Word of God.

It's pretty easy to build a case for what *seems* right. The Bible says that there is a way that seems right to men, but it ends up destroying them. The main thing to remember when weighing our perspective against God's is that His ways are different from ours. His ways are also higher than ours in terms of the bigger picture. What may seem right for the moment to us may be absolutely wrong given the broader application that only God can see. Proverbs states that men must not lean on their own understanding, but must in all their ways defer to the supremacy of God's leadership (Proverbs 3:5-6).

Satan knows that if he can get mankind to buy into what *feels* or *seems* right, he can manipulate them into a grand scheme that will cause the ruination of many souls. Would you agree that it worked for him in the Garden of Eden? Eve actually thought she was doing something good for her and Adam! We're still paying for her failure to depend on God's warning rather than follow her own reasoning. Think of the impact on humanity that her desire for a seemingly harmless, delicious-looking piece of fruit has wrought! She reasoned that it would make her closer to God by making her more like God. Instead, it separated her from God both spiritually and physically.

How many time-honored religious systems have been concocted based on what seems reasonable to their founders? The simple answer is that all religious systems where Jesus is not considered to be God are errant in their fundamental bases. Even when one factors in the great depth of humanitarianism displayed by many highly commendable religious groups, there still remains only one way to eternal life with God in heaven. Belief systems built on any foundations other than

Jesus Christ as God the Son must stop aligning themselves with Christianity. If their proponents say they are Christian, they are apostate. If they proclaim any other way to eternal life than by trusting in the cleansing and atoning blood of the Lamb of God, they are heretical.

Is Christianity the only belief system upheld by God? Absolutely! Jesus is the Way *to* God, the Truth *about* God's love, and the Life *in* God! Those who profess this belief during the window of time known as the Age of Grace shall receive eternal life. During this Age the Holy Spirit of God is in those who believe. In turn, those who believe have the power of God to share the Gospel throughout the earth. When the Holy Spirit within believers is withdrawn from the earth at the moment of the rapture, the power to believe will also be withdrawn from Gentiles as the Age of Grace comes to a close.

CHAPTER SIX

SATAN'S PLANS

As the night fast approaches, and with it the withdrawal of the light of the world (Matthew 5:14), Satan is faced with a real problem. How is he going to dupe a multitude of people into believing that God's Word concerning the end of the Age of Grace is not true? Will he play on the sympathies of church members concerning their loved ones who have not accepted Christ? Will he encourage the more learned scholars to come up with a loophole that seems logical and incontestable? Will he urge the more creative types to develop charts and time lines pointing to an exact day and hour of the second appearing of Christ? Will he inspire members of Satanic cults to rally a campaign denouncing the rapture altogether? I believe that Satan is much more ingenious in his ability to misdirect than any of these tactics might suggest.

According to the Word of God, Satan can appear as an angel of light. His ideals can also appear as a guiding light for church members who are not completely grounded in the Word of God. In fact, some of Satan's most sinister plots to deceive lost church members and casual church attendees have been presented through highly respected clergymen! Some of the giants in the field of Theology have offered up differing viewpoints as to both the time and the events surrounding the end of the Age of Grace. Some will declare emphatically that the Age of Grace on earth will never end!

The thing that Satan will most likely try to conceal from mankind is the Scriptural concept of a thousand-year reign on earth by the returning Jesus Christ. The primary reason may be that during that thousand-year reign, Satan will be bound in a pit, according to the Scriptures. Let the reader be aware that the Prince of Darkness has been preparing for the Lord's return much more vigilantly than any Christian! He has been deceiving the minds of religious leaders for centuries in a carefully scripted manner as preparation for the end of the Age of Grace. He knows better than any human what the Word of God says. It is his task to so muddle the minds of men that they will accept all kinds of varying ideas concerning the coming catastrophe. His best plan is to divide and conquer!

Let's consider that there are at least three distinct millennial concepts espoused by world-class theologians. The *Millennium* is commonly referred to by this author and other Pre-Millennialists as the thousand-year reign of Christ on earth. Most of this chapter will be concerned with the pre-millennial perspective. The word *pre-millennial* suggests that Jesus will return to earth before He sets up His literal thousand-year reign. Other perspectives will be covered in the next chapter.

The Millennial Age covers the time when Jesus and His believers will reign together on the earth following His second coming. The second coming of Jesus is not to be confused with His second appearing. Jesus will *appear* to those who are raptured seven years before His return to the earth. At His second coming, Jesus will return to the earth accompanied by an army of angels and all of the redeemed who were raptured seven years earlier. He will then begin His millennial reign on earth.

The second appearing of Jesus, according to most in the pre-millennial group, will occur at the time of the rapture. According to Scripture, Jesus will reappear in the clouds to those who are being resurrected and to those whose bodies have been altered to accommodate the spiritual realm of heaven. In short, the dead in Christ will be resurrected and joined in the air by the instantly transformed believers who are alive at that time.

After the rapture all believers will be with Jesus for what those who remain on earth will perceive as a time period of seven years. It is important for us to note that there is a different concept of time in heaven. Therefore, from their unique perspective, believers in Christ could experience the rapture and then possibly could immediately return with Jesus to enter into His millennial rule on the earth. In other words for those who have been taken out of the earth's time continuum by the rapture, though seven years will go by on earth, no time will seem to have elapsed in the heavenly realm. For the creator of time the past, present, and future exist simultaneously and continually. Thus we have an example of how '*with God a day is as a thousand years*'.

When Christians first hear that there will be seven years of tribulation following the rapture, there is a tendency for most to begin wondering exactly what those who are raptured will be doing in heaven for those seven earthly years. If people are not careful, there is a temptation for believers to spend needless hours imagining and discussing a scenario that is impossible to comprehend. The topic also can give rise to fantastic mental projections of those very imaginative types who can dream up extraordinary visions of what Christians will be doing in heaven. Is there any real harm in projecting our own imaginings concerning what we will be doing in heaven during the seven years that the Bible does not address? A good rule of thumb concerning arguable topics is simply that, when the Bible is silent on a certain issue, it should be construed that it is not for men to know the times or seasons which the Father has put in His own authority (Acts 1:7).

The danger of projecting human ideas onto a heavenly scenario lies in the unadvised act of creating speculative doctrines as to the purpose of believers after the rapture. In fact, it is the combining of the two terms *speculate* and *Scripture* that has created many of the man-made doctrines under which most denominations and all cults now labor in vain. Worst of all, any type of fantasizing that hinders or supplants one's drive to accomplish the mission of global evangelization in keeping with the Lord's Great Commission for the church must be viewed as unproductive. Why worry or even wonder about the Lord's post-rapture provision for His church? Fortunately, though it is human to worry and wonder, we can gain consolation in the knowledge that time won't really matter for raptured believers.

Following the rapture, the Holy Spirit will be absent from the earth. Those seven years will be a time during which the power of the Holy Spirit that convicts of sin and supplies the truth of God will also be absent. Humanism will reign apart from the influence of the Holy Spirit of God. Though there are many religions that consider their proponents to be holy, we will consider only God's holiness for valid confirmation of the term. Any absence of God's holiness results in ungodliness and, eventually, complete lawlessness. Therefore, the stage will be set for the rise of a charismatic, super dictator, revealed in Scripture as the Antichrist, or *man of lawlessness.* He will bring to bear supernatural powers that will be supplied to him by Satan. Thus he will become the celebrated savior of the world, a title he will sport during the first three and a half years of the tribulation period.

All nations will yield to his authority under a one-world government. However, at the mid-point of the seven years the man of lawlessness, or Antichrist, will unabashedly proclaim that *he is God* (2 Thessalonians 2:4). He will command that all people worship him as God. Those who refuse to acknowledge his deity will face elimination. They will be denied the ability to purchase the necessities of life. Ultimately they will be imprisoned and executed.

When the Antichrist announces that he is God, he will be standing in the reconstructed temple at Jerusalem. At that moment the Jews, who are still awaiting the first appearance of the Messiah, will reject the deity of the Antichrist. This will lead to the increased persecution of the Jews by all of the world powers, and Israel will be threatened with extinction. This hyper-persecution will bring about worldwide preparation for the Battle of Armageddon. The battle will occur seven years after the rapture. Prior to this remarkable battle, the combined armed forces of the world will gather on the plains of Megiddo near Jerusalem in preparation for a battle with Israel. According to Scriptures the battle will pit the Armies of the East (Islamic and Oriental) and the Armies of the West against Jerusalem. The Western Army will be headed by the leaders of Russia and European nations. The Commanders and Kings of the unholy coalition will have been possessed by demons. Under the direction of Satan they will gather outside of Jerusalem for the purpose of completely annihilating Israel. (Revelation 16:16-21).

At this battle of Armageddon Jesus, His angels, and His believers will return to earth just in time to defeat all the enemies of Israel for the preservation of the Jews, the covenant people of God. After the brief but bloody battle, Jesus and His believers will begin the millennial reign over those on the earth who have survived the tribulation. Angels of the Lord will bring all of His elect, the Jews, from the four corners of the earth.

Precisely what that millennial reign will be like is impossible to tell for lack of Scriptural references. However, one thing is clear. It will be an era of unparalleled peace about which we know very little. Satan will be bound for a thousand years, and thus unable to tempt men and governments. The Bible refers to a time when Christians will reign with Christ. The

Scriptures reveal that believers will judge nations and angels (I Corinthians 6:2-3). Believers are referred to in Scripture as *joint heirs with Christ*. Without knowing the details as to how we are to function in those relative positions, suffice it to say that it will be something heavenly!

We must engage ourselves in an exercise of faith by accepting God's Word that whatever else the exact role of believers may be in the millennial rule, it will most certainly be in direct proportion to our faithfulness to the commands of Christ before the rapture. The Apostle Paul wrote that our minds are simply incapable of conceiving the glorious scope of all that God has planned for those who love Him! Neither should we waste our valuable kingdom time on quests involving raw speculation. During our temporary lives on earth we have been sanctified; set apart to do service for the Lord until His reappearing. That service must focus on the primary functions of sharing the Gospel with the lost and discipling those who come to believe in Jesus. After our lives on this planet, we can be sure that our glorified bodies will continue to serve the Lord's best interests forever. Hallelujah!

Allow me to recap at this point in your reading. As mentioned, most Pre-Millennialists believe that Jesus will rapture His Church out of the world before the seven-year period of tribulation that ends with the Battle of Armageddon and the millennial reign of Jesus on earth. Most Pre-Millennialists believe that Paul is referring to the Holy Spirit when he wrote about God's *removal of the restraining force*. The Holy Spirit is that force that is holding back the man of lawlessness during this current Age of Grace. When the influence of the Holy Spirit is removed, those who remain on earth can expect more than a few horrifying results.

When all the believers are removed, it is reasonable to declare that the Holy Spirit inside all believers will also be removed. That occurrence is called the Rapture of the Church! Both the Bride of Christ and the Holy Spirit within the Bride will be raptured. To suggest that the Holy Spirit, or restraining force, could be removed and the believers could remain on earth negates the doctrine concerning the work of the Spirit. Believers are sealed by the Holy Spirit, who was sent by Jesus to be our comforter and our spiritual conscience. If the force that seals our redemption and guides us in all truth is suddenly removed from within us, how then shall we be faithful to the commands of Christ?

The Apostle Paul wrote that believers serve as the temple of the Holy Spirit. Indeed, how shall we continue to be the temple of the Holy Spirit if the Spirit is removed from within us, His temple? If it is the Holy Spirit that sustains our relationship to the Father, what would our relationship to the Father become in lieu of His departed Spirit? Without the convicting power of the Holy Spirit, how would we know to confess and repent of our sins? How would we be different from the unregenerate people on the earth?

There is a simple answer to all of these questions. When Jesus reappears, the Holy Spirit will be evacuated from the earth. Because the Holy Spirit has become an integral part of the believers whom He has sealed unto redemption, they will likewise vacate the earth. Following that event, the earth will indeed be as wicked as it was in the days of Noah before the flood. The one exception will be that there will be no one like Noah left behind! Consequently, with the removal of both the Holy Spirit and the Christian witness of believers, there will be no godly force to restrain the powers of evil that will be unleashed without restraint upon the population of the earth.

In keeping with the opinion of most Christian theologians, the *salt* and *light* effects of Christianity currently limit the forces of darkness from completely overwhelming the earth today. Paul wrote that Christians do not struggle against the flesh (fellow humans), but against rulers, authorities, powers of the dark world, and spiritual forces of evil in the heavenly realms (Ephesians 6:12). He was referring to the influence exerted on humans by the power of Satan, the prince of the air, and his legions of demonic principalities.

CHAPTER SEVEN

MILLENNIAL GROUPS

Several Old Testament and New Testament Scriptures refer to a thousand-year reign of Jesus on the earth. Because of various doctrinal differences, there have arisen at least three distinctly differing perspectives concerning Christ's millennial reign. As stated in the previous chapter the Pre-Millennial view is that the return of Jesus to earth will occur immediately prior to a literal thousand-year reign. The Post-Millennial view holds that Jesus will return *after* a thousand-year reign of the Church. The A-Millennial view maintains that there is no literal thousand-year reign of Jesus in the future. However, there are differing camps of A-Millennialists. One camp believes that the Church is now enjoying a "Messianic Age" with the rule of the political church body serving as Christ-in-proxy. In a more extreme case, some say there will be no literal millennial reign of Jesus Christ on earth. Each of these views will be briefly discussed.

The first group for discussion holds the same view as this author. Pre-Millennialists believe that the Scriptures point to the reappearing of Jesus in a future event called the rapture. The rapture is the "taking up" of all believers (buried or alive) from the earth. Both the dead in Christ and those who are alive will be given new spiritual bodies by which they can ascend into the air to meet Jesus. Following this taking-up activity, the earth will barely endure seven years of severe tribulation.

During the tribulation period the Antichrist, a man possessed by Satan, will pull the world's governments together under his celebrated rule. Equipped by Satan, with great miracles and signs he will convince the nations to ally with him to form a one-world government. Great prosperity will be the result for a period of three-and-a-half years. After that time, the Antichrist will enter the temple at Jerusalem and proclaim that he is God! The Jews will reject this notion and become instant enemies of all the nations.

For the next three-and-a-half years the Jews and anyone else who will not bow to the lordship of the Antichrist will face great persecution. Everyone on earth will be commanded to receive a mark which will allow them to buy and sell. Because of the technical aspects of the mark, every move anyone makes will be known by the head of the new world government. Those who reject the mark will be tortured and killed.

Finally, toward the close of the seven year period, the Antichrist and the heads of other nations will gather on the plains of Megiddo near Jerusalem for the purpose of the annihilation of Israel. The stage will be set for the return of the Lord Jesus in defense of Israel. As the world's armies reach Jerusalem, the Lord will descend from heaven with His holy army of angels and those who have been raptured. Jesus will defeat the enemies of Israel in a battle so fierce that a river of the blood of the enemy will reach a depth of five feet! After the defeat of the Antichrist and the world's armies, Satan and his demons will be thrown into a pit and incarcerated there for a thousand years. During that period, Jesus and His saints will reign during a millennium of peace throughout the world.

Within the Pre-Millennial group are at least three sub-sects. These are the pre-tribulation, mid-tribulation, and post-tribulation thinkers. They all believe in the rapture of the church before the actual return of Jesus, but disagree on the point at which the rapture will occur. Some, including this author, believe it will be before the seven years of tribulation (pre-tribbers). Others believe the rapture will occur at the three-and-a-half-year point (mid-tribbers). And still others believe that the rapture will occur at the end of the tribulation (post-tribbers) and immediately preceding the second coming of Jesus. All of those who embrace Pre-Millennialism are called dispensational eschatologists.

Another millennial perspective is held by a group called A-Millennialists. This group does not believe in the literal millennial reign of Jesus Christ. They also deny the occurrence of the rapture. As a group they are also divided in opinion as to whether Christ will literally return! Most support the doctrine of a "Church Age" or "Messianic Age" during which the Church will rule in the place of Christ as "Christ on Earth" or "Christ-in-Proxy." They refer to the time in which we now live as the millennium.

A-Millennialists embrace at least two "replacement doctrines." They believe that, because of Israel's rejection of

Jesus as the Messiah, the nation has been replaced as God's covenant people by the New Testament Church. They also believe that Christ, Himself, has been replaced by the Church as a "Christ-in-Proxy." Christ becomes to them a figurehead of time and history and, therefore, unattached to current earthly happenings. In fact, they rarely use the name 'Jesus' but almost always refer to Him as 'Christ.' They view the Jewish nation as a people dispossessed by God with no right of inclusion in the eternal kingdom. They refer to the New Testament church as the new Israel, chosen by God.

It is easy to see some of the problems that arise from such a doctrine. In the place of Jesus reigning during an era of peace, the church becomes the ultimate decision-maker in doctrinal creation and the final authority in Scriptural interpretation. For example, A-Millennial adherents such as the Roman Catholic Church exercise final authority over the Word of God. In such a scheme the Roman Catholic Church is guilty of usurping the sovereignty of God's dominion by placing church rule under a dominion granted by the church to a man.

It is not surprising that reformed groups (such as Calvinists) have held on to the A-Millennial perspective embraced by the Roman Catholic Church from which they split during the Protestant Reformation. Though reformers may argue that their doctrines are not affected by their A-Millennial perspective, I submit that they are. A-Millennialists believe that during this *Church Age* the church will benefit from increased inroads into the world's political scheme. They believe that social, political, ecological, and spiritual life on this planet will continually improve instead of decaying. Therefore, since the church is growing in strength, and since society will eventually be ruled by the church, there is little or no zeal for Great Commission evangelism. The lack of evangelistic fervor is also a result of their doctrine of predestination which poses that only a very few chosen people have been created with the ability to accept Christ as Savior and Lord. The rest have been predestined by God for hellfire.

Not the least of social ramifications, A-Millennialists embrace the wholesale replacement of the Jewish nation as God's chosen and covenant people. Imagine how someone under such an ideal could view Jews as worthy of extinction. Also imagine that those with this mindset could easily believe they are simply carrying out God's judgment on Israel by taking part in the holocaust. Considering this doctrine, it is easy to see where anti-Semitic ideals have arisen. At the heart of A-Millennialism is the idea of the reign of man through the church, thus setting up a human kingdom apart from the input of the Living God.

Unlike the Pre-Millennialists the A-Millennialists embrace a belief system where the church is gradually evolving into the spiritual and political ruler of the world. Other differences are seen in the treatment of the Holy Scriptures. A-Millennialists are blind to the Biblical view of essential Christian doctrines such as the rapture, the resurrection of the dead, and the literal return and rule of the Lord of Lords and King of Kings as prophesied in many Scripture passages. Of course, since they believe that they now have authority over the Scriptures, all Scripture is up for reinterpretation so as to aid them in what could seem like their delusion.

Some A-Millennialists, however, believe that the Lord will eventually return to earth, and that will be the end of the age. Some of the great theologians at the turn of the Twentieth Century were avowed A-Millennialists. The list includes presidents and founders of great conservative theological seminaries. It has been suggested that the horrors of the world wars greatly affected the ideology of the A-Millennialists and likewise, greatly diminished the number of proponents. Indeed, how could the world seem to be improving in the face of the constant threat of warring nations? When one considers the millions who have died in war and as a result of famine, meteorological catastrophe, and pestilence since the beginning of the Twentieth Century, it is hard to imagine that life on earth is getting better! Of course, if you believe that those who have perished did so at the delight of their Creator for His own purposes, you might be emboldened in your reformed perspectives.

A different kind of A-Millennialist group is called the Preterists. Preterists believe that all Bible prophecies, including those concerning the Second Coming of Jesus, the Resurrection of the Dead, the Rapture, the Judgment, and the arrival of the Kingdom of God were fulfilled in or around 70 A.D. after the destruction of Herod's temple in Jerusalem. Preterists interpret several passages in the twenty-first chapter of Luke as predictions made by Jesus concerning the coming of judgment to the nation of Israel in 70 A.D. Preterists believe that we are now living in the "new heaven and new earth." They maintain that there is no bodily resurrection, and that nothing remains to be fulfilled prophetically.

The Preterists hold to an allegorical or symbolic interpretation of the Scriptures. When an historical approach is taken, the Preterists must bow out gracefully. They must overlook much strong evidence that supports a futurist or dispensationalist view point. They obviously believe that so few were raptured in or around 70 A.D. that those who missed the rapture never noticed those who were missing! Likewise, they must believe that the Apostle John, who wrote to the churches after 70 A.D. must have either missed the rapture or was given special dispensation!

Preterists must also rule out the current era as the "Times of the Gentiles" spoken of by Jesus in His Great Temple discourse. In Luke 21:24 we see that the "Times of the Gentiles" (what this author believes to be the Age of Grace) must come between the destruction of the temple and the second-coming of Jesus. Can we believe that the Preterists are correct in their understanding of Second Peter? According to their interpretation the earth has already been destroyed by fire! Let the reader understand that this author disagrees aggressively with such a mystical, allegorical view of Scripture.

By far one of the most ridiculous renderings of the various A-Millennial views comes from an avowed Calvinist. His version was captured on DVD during an annual Family Conference in July of 2008. The speaker gave a doctrinal stance heretofore unheard of by this author. He stated on DVD that most people have the idea of the rapture all wrong. He said that instead of the righteous being taken and the unrighteous left behind, it is the other way around! Though he is the pastor of a very large congregation and is a well-known and highly respected motivational speaker, he believes that the wicked will be taken out of the world leaving the righteous to reign. He cites the teachings of Jesus in Matthew about the one being taken and the other being left behind as his proof-text for this new doctrine. Can you believe it?

Can you see how those who believe this new doctrine will certainly be glad to have been left behind at the rapture? (This ideology should prove beyond a doubt that Satan is becoming more aggressive as the Age of Grace comes to a close!)

As mentioned there are differing forms of the A-Millennialist view. Some of the denominations that embrace one or the other of these forms are the United Methodists, the United Presbyterian – USA, Roman Catholics, and some Assembly of God theologians. The bottom line for this perspective is that the idea of a literal return of Jesus followed by His thousand year reign is a ridiculous notion that denies the prophesies of Jesus.

The third group has a Post-Millennial perspective. This group believes that the kingdom of God was established when Jesus was on the earth. They believe that the kingdom is currently spread throughout the world by the sharing of the Gospel and through the saving work of the Holy Spirit. Post-Millennialists maintain that the world will one day be guided by Christian principles and that after a long period of righteousness and peace, Jesus will return. That period is obviously much longer than a thousand years and, therefore, represents a figurative rather than literal millennium.

This group is the most radical of the three groups. They believe that the thousand-year reign has already occurred!

Like the A-Millennialists they refer to the millennium as the "Church Age" during which the church rules in place of Christ as the fulfillment of Scripture. Instead of the belief that a returning Jesus will rule with an iron rod for a thousand-year period of peace and prosperity, they opt for a figurative reign of Christ that already occurred after the early church age.

Frankly this author has never read nor heard of a thousand-year period of time following the ascension of Jesus wherein there was sustained peace and prosperity for the whole world. What we all have read and heard about are the horrors of bloody wars, perilous times of pestilence and famine, manifold sagas of persecution, massive church corruption, and political intrigue. Add to this the Holocaust and several recent cases of national genocide, and tell me things are getting better! These could hardly be the manifestations of a millennial reign of Christ or His church…not even metaphorically! If Satan and his demons were bound during any millennium since the ascension of Jesus, surely it would have been noticeable to someone! Perhaps they are referring to the Pax Romana, or Peace of Rome, when the Roman Empire supposedly governed the world peacefully for a thousand years. (That sounds Catholic to me!)

There are many noted theologians who have espoused the Post-Millennial view. Among them are Eusebius (260-340 A.D.), Augustine (354-430 A.D.), John Calvin, Jonathan Edwards, Matthew Henry, and A. H. Strong. It should be noted that most Post-Millennialists are of the Reformed theological persuasion. This doctrinal stance makes it easy to see why they believe the way they do. Reformed theologians believe that the "elect" will eventually convince the world of their religious beliefs. As the "elect" they are already ruling in the kingdom of God. They also believe everything that happens is according to the express will of God. That includes all manner of sinful activity – even the rape of a child! Although this idea may permit them to sleep better at night, it certainly throws a wet blanket on the loving character of Almighty God!

According to Reformed Theology God chose or "elected" before the creation of the world those who would become believers. Unfortunately, that also means that God chose those who would burn alive in hell forever. Aside from the horrible accusation that the Lord God is the greatest mass-murderer ever to exist, let's consider how such a belief system could systematically set itself up as the millennial ruler of the world in place of Jesus Christ. The reason you will never hear a Post-Millennial preacher giving reference to the tempting power of Satan and his demons is that they believe Satan and his demons are bound during this glorious era. Does it seem to you that Satan has no effect during this current age? Do you think we are living in a wonderful time of peace?

Imagine this. There is a theology today that names God as the reason that most of the people ever created will suffer eternal damnation. This theology also denies that the Word of God names Jesus as the Lamb of God who takes away the sins of the whole world and not just an elect few. It is easy to see how such a system of theology could also easily embrace the notion that the rapidly falling, apostate world of today is actually getting better and more spiritual! The truth is that today people are being deceived by Reformed theological concepts into thinking that they are the "elect" when actually they believe in a false god. Is it any wonder that reformers do not preach about the rapture and the return of Jesus! Most do not believe in either concept!

Many people will ask, "What difference does it make in one's faith perspective if he believes in this millennial concept or that one?" It's really quite simple. Just ask someone if they believe that the devil is operating in the world today. If they say 'no,' you'll know to avoid any further theological discussions with such a kook! Ask them if God created most of mankind for the express purpose of burning alive in hell forever. A 'yes' will expose them as being Reformed and deceived in their theology. Ask them if they believe that man is born without the ability to choose good or evil. If they believe that man wasn't created with free will to choose or reject God, they are reformed in their theology. If they are reformed in their theology, they are most likely A-Millennialists, and therefore believe that they *are* Christ-in-proxy during the current Church Age ruling in the place of the Lord Jesus Christ. They also believe that the world is getting better all the time! Do You?

The most challenging aspect of the millennial discussion is that very few who attend any of the mainline denominational churches have the slightest idea which camp they are in! Most on the membership rolls of mainline denominational churches are happy to remain discompassionate and apathetic with regard to end time ideologies and eternal concepts. While many simply choose not to care what their pastors and church leaders believe, it would behoove all church members to find out what the Bible says about the return of the Lord Jesus.

74

Knowing what your leaders believe about the Second Coming of Jesus and His plan for those who believe in Him is very important. If your church leadership believes that church doctrine supersedes the Word of God in authority, you should begin to seek out a Bible-believing church. If your church leadership believes that all Bible prophesy has been fulfilled as do some A-Millennialists, the Gospel they promote is merely a reformed, social Gospel aimed at improving the planet and not for preparing people spiritually for eternity with Jesus.

A final word about the millennial camps may prove either meaningful or merely comical, depending on your particular camp. Imagine what kind of millennial doctrine Satan might try to invent. He knows what the Word of God says about the return of Jesus. He knows that he and his demons will be bound in a pit for a thousand years during the earthly millennial reign of Jesus. Hmmmm! I submit that he would deceptively infect the more highly enlightened kinds of theological minds with the notion that there is no literal millennial reign. I bet he would also plant deep within the minds of the true religious egotists the notion that there isn't even a literal return of Jesus! Satan might even go so far as to cultivate the idea that he and his demons are *ALREADY BOUND* during the current age! That way there should be no interest in preaching against his destructive and deceitful ways. Why, how can he pose any kind of threat at all since he has been bound during this wonderful Church Age! (Wink, wink!!!)

The fact that there are at least three schools of thought about both the millennial reign of Jesus and the rapture demonstrates how divided a group of well-intending, highly respected theologians can be concerning any particular church doctrine. In fact, it is interesting how splintered the church of Jesus Christ can become over such an issue as the Rapture of the Church! One doesn't have to look very far to see the persona behind such confusion and divisions within the church. This is Satan's greatest plan. Divide and conquer!

As soon as differing viewpoints emerge, it seems that more time is spent by the messengers of the Gospel fighting over semantics than seeking those who are lost! The preaching of the Gospel carries a much greater priority than debating the fine points of the rapture. This book, for instance, is not designed to start arguments about the rapture. The intent of this work is to spur believers onward in their efforts to win the lost while the Age of Grace is in full flower!

CHAPTER EIGHT

SAVED THROUGH FAITH

There are several definitions of the word *faith*.

1. Confidence or trust in a person or thing: Faith in another's ability.
2. Belief that is not based on proof: He had faith that the theory would be substantiated by facts.
3. Belief in God or in the doctrines or teachings of religion: The firm faith of the Pilgrims.
4. Belief in anything, as a code of ethics, standard of merit, etc.: To be of the same faith with someone concerning honesty.
5. A system of religious belief: The Christian faith, the Jewish faith, etc.
6. The obligation of loyalty or fidelity to a person, promise, engagement, etc.: Failure to appear would be breaking faith.

7. The observance of this obligation; fidelity to one's promise, oath, allegiance, etc.: He was the only one who proved his faith during troubles.
8. Christian Theology. Trust in God and in His promises as made through Jesus Christ and the Scriptures by which people are justified or saved.
9. (Idiomatic) In faith or, in truth; indeed: In faith, he is a fine lad.

In this book we will concentrate on definition number five for our application of the word. Christian Faith is belief in Jesus as God, the outward display of which is productive service to Him. Let the reader notice that there are many religious people who generously apply definition number four, whereby all who call themselves Christian have some kind of saving faith. Therefore, there is a great temptation to confuse religious practices with Biblical faith. Jesus pointed out that many of the most religious people in the world will be denied access to heaven because they lacked true, saving faith concerning exactly who Jesus is. Recognizing who Jesus is and responding with total surrender of our lives to Him is the only acceptable means of demonstrating saving faith. Because "faith" is also an action word, each believer must work out his/her faith as the Holy Spirit leads.

How do we apply saving faith to the doctrine of the Rapture of the Church? Beneath all the discussion about the rapture lies an undeniable truth. The rapture will occur at the end of the Age of Grace. The Age of Grace is that time allotted to the Gentiles (non-Jews) during which adoption into the family of God is open to all the nations of the world. However, after the rapture, the world will be void of all Christian influence because it will likewise be void of the sin-convicting power of the Holy Spirit. If we believe that Jesus will soon rapture His church, we will, as the old Gospel song suggests, "Work, for the night is coming!"

During these last days Satan has launched His most menacing and deceptive plot. Since mankind has a more-or-less suspicious nature, most have developed a wait-and-see attitude concerning the rapture. It is Satan's goal to convince people that there will be opportunities to accept Jesus as Lord after the rapture of the church. Using his standard tactics, Satan has drawn support from the emotional types who lean heavily on their own understanding. These crusaders choose to dismiss the Word of God and follow their hearts in laying down a philosophy that makes it possible for people to accept Christ apart from the convicting power of the Holy Spirit. Their main argument centers on the rationale that people who have heard about the rapture will certainly know what has happened after it has occurred. Hmmm! Seems logical, doesn't it?

How great that would be for people like good ol' Uncle Billy. You know Uncle Billy. Every family or church group has one. Even though Uncle Billy neither cared for the church nor darkened the church door step, somehow miraculously he will suddenly see the Gospel message clearly! Uncle Billy will suddenly *know* that all of that *church talk* about Jesus was actually true! He'll fall on his knees, repent to God, and be gloriously saved! Will good old Uncle Billy, who only spoke the name of Jesus when angry or cursing or telling a joke, be able to receive God's grace apart from faith in Jesus? Don't believe it!

In truth Uncle Billy's life will follow an entirely different course. After the rapture, all of the Uncle Billies of the world will find it even *more* difficult to believe in Jesus than they did before the rapture! People are not saved because they *KNOW* what has happened or because they have *SEEN* the truth. Salvation comes by the grace of God only through our *FAITH* in His Word. Salvation is only accomplished by the witness of the Holy Spirit either through a believer or through the Word of God. We are saved by trusting in that which cannot be known or seen. We are saved by grace through FAITH!

Faith in God is accomplished in believers, held by believers, and shared supernaturally through the ministry of the Holy Spirit of God by believers. If you have to *see* the truth to believe it, you will neither see it, nor can you ever believe it! You can only believe without seeing if you have faith. Faith comes by hearing the Word of God!

Many of those who think people will accept Jesus after the rapture are depending on some kind of universal fairness loophole! They imagine that if people call upon the name of the Lord, even after the rapture, they should be saved. Sound fair enough? Actually fairness has little to do with it. It's really more about convenience. Let's suppose people could be saved after the rapture *apart* from the faith that is birthed only by the Holy Spirit. How convenient it would be for those who could never trust in the unseen Savior, but would gladly place their faith in that which they *could* see…that Jesus has, indeed, raptured His church.

When considering what is fair, just consider the millions of believers martyred throughout the Age of Grace because they believed in an unseen Savior. Their eternal reward was sure because of their faith in what they could not see, but supernaturally believed because of the Holy Spirit's witness within them. Uncle Billy may suddenly give assent to the possibility of the rapture of the church, but he will remain on earth because he rejected the witness of the Holy Spirit during the Age of Grace. The question is simple. Should those who have denied and rejected Jesus (because they couldn't see Him) get a convenient second chance after they have seen His rapture? Is this fair to the martyrs who loved their unseen God unto death?

Uncle Billy not only received the urging of the Holy Spirit, his family, and his Christian friends, but he also had the Word of God available to him every day on an unrestricted basis. He had the testimonies of millions of other believers every day of his life. In the face of so great a witness He made the eternal choice to reject Jesus' offer of eternal life. In essence, he called the Holy Spirit a liar. Yes, Uncle Billy will be sad to have been left behind. He will be sad like the thief who thought he had a perfect plan, but then he got caught. He will be sad only because he was left behind and not because of his thoughtless rejection of Jesus.

The Biblical truth is that there will be no Holy Spirit in other believers on earth to convict Uncle Billy of the sin of disbelief. All believers and the Holy Spirit will have been raptured. He may feel like he messed up, but he won't know why! He may even sense that he has lost something, but he won't know what! He most likely will get very angry after he recovers from his brief moment of sadness. As a human intellect with no possible connection to God, most likely his emotions will drive him to a state of rage and rebellion that will cause him to rant and rave against both God and all those who have been raptured. He will in all likelihood shift the blame for his missing heaven to his family, who, in his estimate, should have tried much harder to convert him. Another human characteristic that will arise in him is that of pride. Pride keeps most people from accepting Jesus in the first place.

Think for just a moment how horribly inhumane some people are today who reject the love of God. Now imagine a time when there will be no possibility of a Spirit-guided conscience to monitor the actions and reactions of a person. The closer we get to the rapture the more we are able to see in part what kind of hatred a generation of non-believers is capable of. A recent American survey reveals that of the population born since 1980; forty per cent claim no religious affiliation. This percentage is up significantly from previous decades. It is no surprise that the criminal activity of people within that age group has increased significantly. This does not mean that all non-religious people are criminals, but it shows a rise in lawlessness.

The Bible says that God will honor that nation whose God is the Lord. God has indeed honored the United States of America. One only need look at the rich Christian influence of our founding fathers. Many of the men who framed our Constitution and other guiding documents were decidedly Christian. Their laws and statutes mirrored the Biblical ideals of justice and fairness. With godliness as a governing theme, America has very rapidly risen to the pinnacle of world leadership. This feat was not accomplished by global conquest, but with the goal of helping other nations enjoy God's bountiful provision. Because of her trust in God, America has truly been blessed by the Creator and Provider of Grace. In the face of such provision, should the United States continue to stray from the path carved by her founders, destruction is not only possible, but is promised by the Word of God. Why do I believe America is losing spiritual ground? In a recent survey of Americans professing to be Christians, forty-five percent believed that Jesus was not the only way to the Father! Forty percent of those who professed to be Christians did not believe in Satan or punishment in hell! What do you think?

The reader's mind may have wandered to the fact that you know some non-believers who are very kind and generous. You may know some people who are definitely not Christians but are also not hateful or degenerate in their life-styles. Let's not forget that many of the world's religions foster respect and degrees of tolerance in their teachings. Also, in America, there are those good old boys who would give you the shirt off of their backs, but would never attend church or desire to seem religious. So how will the absence of the Holy Spirit affect these people? They will continue in their kindly life-styles until they are confronted with the horrible situations created by those power-hungry types that will be easy subjects for demonic possession. Without the restraining power of the Holy Spirit people will have no limitations on just how evil they can be! The resulting massive power grabs will turn even the most docile among those left behind into frustrated, angry, and eventually violent people.

Another type of non-religious American is the secular humanist. Although it is a religion, it is really more about personal gain than anything else. These folks are generally nice, well groomed, and non-threatening to average citizens. They do not believe in Jesus as the Savior of the world. Therefore, after the rapture, they will go on being secular humanists just like those in other pagan religions will go on being pagans.

It's not like everyone on earth will suddenly go into a demonic rage after the rapture! However, it will be a time of great tribulation at several levels. Those who do not wish to participate in the one-world governmental system will experience great tribulation. The earth will experience great tribulation due to earthquakes, floods, uncontrollable fires, hurricanes, and other meteorological phenomena. After three and a half years, the Jews will begin to experience great tribulation as they are persecuted for not worshipping the Antichrist.

CHAPTER NINE

FIRST SCENARIO

There have been many full length motion pictures produced by Christian ministries with the goal of showing what life will be like following the rapture. The Christian authors of the screen plays have attempted to be true to their various Scriptural interpretations concerning the rapture. It is my suggestion, however, that most have erred by not pointing out the utter hopelessness that will exist once the Holy Spirit has been removed from the earth. My conclusion is that they do not believe that the Holy Spirit is the restraining force that now prevents the man of lawlessness from taking his post-rapture place as world leader. Therefore, I submit the following scenario as a potential look at what life will be like on earth following the rapture.

When the rapture occurs, it will be exactly as Jesus has described. Two people will be working and one will suddenly disappear without a trace from the view of the other. For the one that remains on the earth the moment will at the very least be startling. Since, according to the Lord's description, the two were working in a field, it will seem impossible for the one remaining to figure out where the other has gone. The raptured person will not slowly dematerialize as is seen in science fiction movies or television programs. According to the Apostle Paul that which will take place will occur in the twinkling of an eye. From the observer's perspective the disappearance of the person raptured will be instantaneous and complete.

Although Jesus said that two people will be sleeping in a bed and one of them will disappear, we should not automatically assume that Jesus will come in the evening or at night. We must remember that there are differing time zones, and that when it is evening in one region on earth, it is morning in another. Suffice it to say that one morning, when many people awaken, their spouse, parent, child, sibling, friend, or significant other will not be in their usual awakening place!

Let's look at a scenario that involves a crowd of people. Strictly for comic relief (although it is not the least bit funny, but embarrassingly unfortunate) let's suppose that the rapture occurs on a Sunday morning. What if it occurs during a worship service of any one of several supposedly Christian denominations? It is highly probable that many church members will not be raptured with the true believers in Christ! How will those who remain react? If the person sitting next to you in the pew suddenly disappeared while you were whispering to him or her, what would you think?

Let's consider a crowd scenario. What about the unsaved passengers on a commuter bus or commercial airplane? If the driver or pilot is a Christian, the controller of the vehicle will suddenly be absent! The passengers will be among the first to experience the deadly horrors of the post-rapture aftermath! Since they were not believers in Jesus and potentially among the first fatalities, their deaths will mark the beginning of their suffering in hell forever. All non-Christian passengers in taxi cabs, cars, trucks, or any other mode of transportation that requires one controller will be at risk, if their drivers are Christians.

Imagine if the rapture occurs at the peak traffic time in New York, Los Angeles, or other highly populated metropolitan areas! It will take hours, or maybe days, to untangle the monstrous traffic jams. Picture unmanned vehicles careening off of bridges and interstate highways or plowing into crowded malls and pedestrians at seventy miles per hour! Automobiles that are driving up steep inclines will zigzag backwards downhill into oncoming traffic. If the rapture occurs at lunchtime in highly populated downtown business areas, unmanned cars will crush thousands of people in crowded crosswalks. If it is at dusk or during the evening commute, the twilight will make it even more difficult for those who missed the rapture to dodge the unmanned, vehicular missiles.

Christian operators of heavy and dangerous equipment also pose a life-threatening hazard to those who either work beside them or happen to be passing nearby. Their sudden disappearance could turn a piece of dangerous power equipment into an unmanned killing machine. Innocent, but not so innocent, bystanders will be injured if not killed by out-of-control power equipment. If airplane traffic controllers or train switch monitors are suddenly not at their stations at crucial moments, the results could be disastrous at metropolitan airplane terminals or train stations.

What about Christians in key leadership positions in the military or federal government? If the President, the Vice president, the Secretary of State, or other key governmental officials are raptured, what would become of the operational and strategic chain of command? We must suppose that of all the high-ranking government officials in Washington D. C. some are bound to be believers! Suddenly many states will be without representation for periods of weeks or months. Highly ambitious senators who missed the rapture will seize all of the governmental committee power that they can while senator-less states attempt to elect new senators. Noticing our scrambling around in a weakened defensive condition, will the ungodly enemies of America combine for a govern-ment coup d'état?

Let's turn our focus to the public school systems. Consider the many trouble-filled classrooms where discipline has been absent since the mid-sixties when God was legislated out of the public schools. Utter chaos will reign when Christian teachers and Principals are suddenly missing from their school board-stifled positions. Lost High School and Middle School students will literally slaughter each other during the pande-monium and ensuing struggles for power. (Though we want to believe that all of the public school teachers in America are Christians, this may not be the case! It certainly is not the case with many college and university professors!)

If a Christian surgeon is performing an intricate procedure on an unregenerate heart patient at the time of the rapture, you can guess what the sad outcome will be for the already unfortunate patient. Likewise, the medical and mental care-givers throughout American society who are Christians will be suddenly and sorely missed by their dependent patients. The patients of those Christian caregivers who dispense vital medicines in exact dosage at precise times will not survive in the absence of their therapeutic administrators.

There are many, many other examples wherein cata-strophic neglect will be realized. Christian garbage men will leave behind messy neighborhoods. Christian policemen who direct traffic will leave behind major traffic jams and violators of traffic laws. Christian military men from every branch of the service, if serving during a time of war, will leave behind both unprotected battle zones and fellow soldiers who will not be able to defend against superior enemy numbers. Christian carnival ride operators will leave behind startled passengers on the rides of their lives! Christian chefs and cooks will leave behind some of the most delicious but soon-to-be completely burnt cuisine.

Probably the worst scenario of all involves lost teenagers of Christian parents. They may return home from school having been released early due to the disappearance of some of their friends and teachers. They may arrive expecting to find their parent. After several hours and many failed attempts to locate them by phone, they will enter the panic zone! Of course getting from the schools to their homes should have already heightened their paranoia. Other students missing, still other students panicking, teachers missing, bus drivers missing, major traffic jams, numerous wrecks, police sirens wailing…and no one has a clue as to what has happened!

The purpose of this chapter has been to mention just a few of the remarkable scenarios that the rapture will produce. The next chapter will deal with why no one will have a clue as to what has taken place following the Rapture of the Church. Brace yourself for some logic that is unearthly in nature. The Bible states that God's ways are different and higher than ours. He is not encumbered by our sense of what seems right. In fact, the Bible says that there is a way that seems right to man, but the end thereof is death! (Proverbs 14:12) God has already seen what will happen after He removes His Holy Spirit from the realm of the earth. Mankind, complete with big, emotional hearts that are constantly tempted by Satan to seek the way that may seem right, can never be godly enough in this life to second guess God. This book will show by using the Word of God that the world will not have a clue as to what has happened regarding those who have been raptured.

CHAPTER TEN

THE HOLY SPIRIT'S ROLE
ON EARTH

As mentioned before, no one on earth knows the exact day or hour of the reappearing of the Lord in the air. We can count on this truth because Jesus said it (Matthew 24:36). In the Word of God, Jesus states definitely, metaphorically, and categorically that there will be a rapture of His church. We know that in the days of Noah God delivered the only true believers in Him from the flood. He will also deliver the believers in Jesus from the soon-coming, flood of terror known as the Great Tribulation. God will initiate the Great Tribulation Period by the removal of His Holy Spirit from the earth. At this point it is important to explain that the word tribulation is not applied to believers. Jesus said that in this world believers would have tribulation, but that we should not fear because He has overcome the world (John 16:33). This form of tribulation is not the same as that which is referred to in the phrase *the Great Tribulation*. The term *Great Tribulation* applies to the earth and those who remain on it after the rapture. It designates perilous events that will be more catastrophic than ever before in earth's history (Matthew 24:21).

The fact that believers are even interested in what will occur on the earth after their rapture may be puzzling to students of the Word. The only point of concern on the part of believers should be the sad truth that Gentiles who are not born-again believers in Jesus may miss sharing His glory forever when they miss the rapture. I say "*MAY* miss sharing His glory" because not all of the Gentile inhabitants of the earth will die during the tribulation. Some will make it through, and they will see the Second Coming of Jesus. Thus, they will have a chance during His thousand-year reign on earth to accept Him as Lord.

Therefore, of prime interest to all believers should be the evangelization of the world beginning right where we live. Our lifestyles of evangelism must continue right up to the time we either pass from this realm by physical death or are raptured at Jesus' reappearing. To be concerned about what will happen to those who have rejected Christ only serves to second guess the judgment of the Lord Himself. Does He not know about those who will be left behind? Will He somehow slip up and not give everyone a chance to respond to the Gospel message before He calls His church out of this realm? The answer lies in the Word of God. God is righteous and just!

Jesus said that His Gospel will be preached to the entire world and then the end will come (Matthew 24:14). This means that our wonderfully righteous and always just God knows the exact moment of the end of the Age of Grace. Jesus has commanded the preaching of the Gospel to all of the Gentile nations (Matthew 28:19). The Age of Grace is the time period during which His command will be carried out. The Jews are truly God's covenant people. Their uniqueness concerning the period of tribulation will be addressed later. However, remember that it was soon after the Jews' overwhelming rejection of the Son of God that Jesus commissioned His disciples to the task of global evangelization.

Jesus has commissioned His church to offer the gift of eternal life to all people everywhere. To enable His church to carry out this awesome task, Jesus sent His Holy Spirit to live inside His believers. The purpose of the Holy Spirit is many fold. He is our companion in the absence of Jesus. He guides us in all truth concerning the Word of God. He enables us to recall the Word of God in times of trials and tribulations. He also convicts the world of sin and is the convincing force concerning the truth that Jesus is God. Jesus said that the Holy Spirit *clothes* us with power from heaven, and we will be His witnesses to the whole earth (Acts 1:8). Jesus also promises that everyone who believes the Gospel will receive the same Holy Spirit, and likewise be empowered to testify about Jesus concerning salvation from sin.

Jesus told His first disciples that they would be delivered up to be tried in various courts for their belief in Him. He told them that they need not worry about what to say during those trials, but that the Holy Spirit would provide them with Words from heaven. Jesus was so emphatic about His teaching on the purpose of the Holy Spirit that He told His disciples not to attempt any evangelism whatsoever before being empowered from on high with the Holy Spirit (Acts 1:4,5).

After Jesus ascended into heaven, about one hundred and twenty believers waited together in a house for the dramatic arrival of the Holy Spirit. They prayed together in an upper room as they waited for the promise of the Lord. They did not know the day or the hour of the coming of the Holy Spirit. (Neither will the believers of today know the day or the hour of His departure, and ours in the rapture!) On the Day of Pentecost they were still together in the upper room waiting and praying as Jesus had instructed. It makes me wonder how many glorious things believers miss from God today by shortening their revival efforts to a mere week or even a mere four evenings together! Jesus said to pray, so they prayed together…expectantly. Jesus said to wait, and so they waited together…expectantly!

Finally, seven weeks after Jesus' ascension into heaven, the moment arrived. The believers were there in that upper room together…waiting and praying as instructed. Suddenly, there occurred what the writer of Acts describes as the sound of a mighty rushing wind. We have seen enough news footage of hurricanes and viewed enough movies about great wind storms to imagine the awesome sound of the coming of the 'breath of God.' However, we have no way of imagining the eerie spectacle of what the Bible describes as cloven tongues of fire appearing from nowhere and resting on the heads of all those present! The departure of the Holy Spirit of God from this earth will be no less spectacular as believers are swept up into the presence of Jesus!

Because the Bible uses the word *tongues* in the description of the fire, many Pentecostal Christians assume that the coming of the Holy Spirit into a person's life will be manifested by them speaking in some kind of unknown dialect or 'tongues.' In other words, many Pentecostals believe that a person is not eternally secure *(saved)* unless he or she is filled with the Holy Spirit, the manifestation of which is speaking in unknown tongues. Some Pentecostal denominations even offer classes in speaking in unknown tongues!

It is interesting to note that the unknown tongues spoken by the disciples were indeed languages and dialects that were unknown to them, but known to people from other regions. The Bible attests to the fact that the disciples were heard glorifying God in languages that were only known by people from foreign lands. Such a supernatural display of the power of the Holy Spirit would have made it hard for the disciples of Jesus not to grasp the meaning of their speaking in foreign tongues! They were sure to remember that Jesus had told them to *go to all nations and make disciples!* This manifestation should have driven home the truth that they were indeed able to go and make disciples of all nations with the help of the Holy Spirit sent by Jesus for that purpose.

The assertion that in order to receive eternal life one must speak in a language that is not known to anyone on earth is blasphemy of the Holy Spirit! It is undoubtedly a doctrine of man and not of God. It suspiciously points to a works-based faith system. Salvation is by grace through faith and not of works. It is the gift of God (Ephesians 2:8). The coming of the Holy Spirit and the subsequent witness of the disciples to people from differing linguistic areas was simply the supernatural indication that the Gospel was for *all people*. Incidentally, the language normally used to describe fire and its effects contains the term *tongues,* as in the phrase, *"The fiery tongues licked at the building!"*

The coming of the Holy Spirit marked the beginning of the Age of Grace. Each of the Disciples of Christ was filled with the Holy Spirit of God. Therefore, each believer was equipped for the task of global evangelization. Make no mistake about it. Either Christians have a witness or testimony concerning the love of Jesus that has resulted in their salvation, or they are not Christians at all! The possibility of being a believer and not being filled with the power of the Holy Spirit to testify concerning the love of God is contradictory to the purpose of both the believer and the Holy Spirit. Even so, a person could visit hundreds of churches and run into thousands of so-called believers who have never shared their testimonies with lost people. The saddest true example is the elderly man who sports a thirty-five year Sunday School perfect-attendance pin, but has never witnessed to a lost person!

A person who claims to be a Christian is at the same time claiming to be filled with the Holy Spirit. No one desires to obey the commands of Jesus unless he or she is filled with the Holy Spirit. On the other hand, those who are filled with the Holy Spirit have not only the desire to please God through obedience to His commands, but also the supernatural power to be His witnesses to the ends of the earth, beginning where they live. Without the Holy Spirit abiding in the hearts of people, there is neither the desire nor the power to obey the commands of Jesus.

Imagine what kind of treacherous, lawless, merciless world would exist without the presence of the Holy Spirit. The Bible describes the state of mind of those who have been filled with the Holy Spirit. Their common attitudes are described as fruit of the Spirit. Spirit-filled believers are known by their actions and reactions. They exhibit love, joy, peace, patience, kindness, goodness, faithfulness, gentleness and self-control (Galatians 5:22). Their responses to the bumps and knocks of life on earth are considered strange to those who are governed by their passions and life's circumstances.

Jesus taught His disciples to live in accordance with kingdom principles. He also was the perfect role model for righteous actions and reactions. However, Jesus also knew that His followers would not be able to live up to kingdom standards apart from the influence of His Holy Spirit from within each one of them. Even Christians are capable of acting on their emotions apart from the guidance of the Holy Spirit. When it is all said and done, believers will always have to choose whether to listen to the still, small, righteous voice of the Holy Spirit of God or whether to obey their own passions. When Christians pursue their own earthly appetites, they run the risk of grieving the Holy Spirit. When a person finds that he or she is constantly obeying self instead of the Spirit's urgings, his or her relationship with Jesus needs Biblical re-evaluation and spiritual restoration.

The Bible states that a true child of God cannot continue in a lifestyle of sinfulness (1 John 3:9). When Christians sin, it is the Holy Spirit who reminds them through conviction. It is also the Holy Spirit who prompts them to confess and repent of their sins. Without the Holy Spirit, none of this will happen. If people are brought up by parents who at least know right from wrong, they will most likely be able to make good, moral decisions whether they are believers or not. However, they will never be able to make godly decisions that result in souls being saved apart from the presence of God's Holy Spirit in their lives.

The next chapter deals with the kinds of awful things that will happen to non-believers after the rapture. Hopefully those who are very concerned about family members or friends who are not believers will be able to chart a new course of action concerning them. Believers should develop a new perspective on the hopelessness that the world will face apart from the Holy Spirit's influence. Hopefully, this will encourage and motivate many lukewarm believers to redouble our efforts to spread the Good News!

CHAPTER ELEVEN

STORY I: THE UNCHURCHED

Jesus said the last days would be like the days before Noah and his family entered the ark (Matthew 24:38). Imagine the depth of sin and depravity God must have seen during those days! Such unbridled sin and chaos ultimately led to His decision to wipe out all of mankind except Noah's family. Jesus, as God the Son, observed those days of wanton moral depravity and the blatant lawlessness of wicked mankind. The period of time from Adam to Noah was a little over a thousand years. Adam was alive for most of that time. He, too, saw the generations of his offspring sink deeper and deeper into their immoral, selfish ways. God was so disgusted with the sinfulness of Adam's race that He decided to begin anew. He noticed that Noah practiced love for Him as the world's only righteous man.

We must agree, however, that God knew before He created the earth, that most of Adam's race will immerse themselves into the depths of sinfulness. Even so, God is not reactive like us. Because He is omniscient, God saw every moment of man's future history before He created the world. You can also be sure that God foreknew all that is ever going to happen in each of our lives. The Bible reveals to us that though we each have a choice to do good or evil, very often God takes a personal and obvious hand in His dealings with us. It's great to know that when evil men exert their own wills to place us in harm's way, God is watching over His own. We can be sure that miracles are happening all the time — many that we are never even aware of.

Throughout the Old Testament we see God intervening in the lives of people who were very important to His Messianic plan. God's Spirit moved externally upon Bible heroes through the performance of great miracles. During the Age of Grace, however, the Holy Spirit has been given to all believers by Jesus, and He performs His purposes internally. Believers have wonderful counsel available 24/7 from within our hearts as God's Spirit communes with ours. This communion will never end. When believers are raptured out of this atmosphere, the Holy Spirit will accompany them into the presence of the Lord. The new bodies of believers will be spiritual, like the new, ascended body of Jesus.

Quite literally, the Holy Spirit will not tarry on the earth after the rapture. The Age of Grace will have ended. Unless God decides to apply the power of the Holy Spirit in the external affairs of those who remain on earth, men will be left with neither a moral compass, nor an internal convicting foundation. Just as in the days of Noah before the flood, a time of extreme lawlessness and immorality is returning. The Bible states that the time of great tribulation on earth will begin when the restraining force is removed. Even now God's Holy Spirit restrains the world's forces of wickedness. When the rapture occurs, the Holy Spirit will be removed and, consequently, there will be nothing to restrain iniquity on the earth.

Perhaps the most bizarre reality will be the sudden disappearance of many people. As previously mentioned, Christians will be *snatched away* in the twinkling of an eye (1 Thessalonians 4:17)! Those who are in a position to observe the manner of departure will have no idea what happened! One way to address the instantaneous rapture of believers is to provide a probable situation.

Two young women, Heather and Amy, have just parked in a parking lot and are walking toward the ticket booth of a local movie theater. They are carrying on their usual lively conversation in eager anticipation of the movie they have waited all week to see. Amy is laughing as she looks at Heather and jokes about the fact that they are going to a movie without dates. Suddenly, while Amy is in the middle of her chuckle, Heather disappears from view. Amy finishes her snickering even though there is no one listening. It takes her a couple of seconds to process the fact that Heather is no longer where she was just an instant ago! In a spontaneous physical reaction Amy looks to the left and then to the right. She then turns in a full circle looking for her best friend, who is nowhere to be seen.

Realizing she is alone, Amy begins to call out, "Heather? Heather! Now where did she go?"

After another few seconds, with her hands on her hips Amy looks out across the parking lot toward the car from which they came. Just then, her attention is captured by a man frantically searching between the cars in the parking lot. She hears him shouting out two names. The sounds of his calling grow dimmer as he turns the corner and disappears behind the theater. All of this action seems to be taking place in slow motion due to the bizarre sense of confusion that is beginning to take a toll on Amy. Intuitively, she begins to realize that something is terribly wrong!

She whispers, "Wait a minute. Am I having some kind of *twilight zone* moment?" As Amy's heart rate quickens and her level of panic rises, so does her sense of denial.

Because there is no rational explanation for what seems to have happened, she begins to question herself, "Heather *was* with me tonight…wasn't she?"

Maybe she only thought Heather was with her. Subconsciously she begins to adapt to the emerging defense mechanism known as *denial.* She imagines that her friend is probably still at her own house.

"Sure! That's it!" She says, trying to convince herself of something that she's still not sure of. Their trip to the movies must have been scheduled for another evening that week.

She suddenly shakes her head, stomps her foot and blurts out, "Then… why am I here?"

Her well-organized mind fights to create every kind of scenario to dismiss the reality of what obviously has taken place. She finds her cell phone and stares at the numbers pad. What if she calls Heather and she's not at home? What will she tell her mom? Where is Heather?

She then mutters to herself in halting words, "People can't just disappear!"

In the next moment Amy's apprehension begins to soar as all of the theater doors burst open and people pour hysterically onto the sidewalk and stream into the parking lot. The look of panic on the faces of those running through the parking lot raises the intensity of horror in her stunned mind. The previously quiet sidewalk has become more like a department store during a huge Christmas sale! The roar of shuffling feet and the voices of people calling out names reminds Amy of her High School hallway at the end of the last day of school. However, instead of extreme elation she flinches at the terror-widened eyes of strangers frantically searching the faces of those who are running along beside them.

As the clamor increases Amy realizes that something truly bizarre has definitely happened to a number of people, including her best friend.

"Heather! Heather!" she joins the shouting of the horrified people in the maddening scene developing around her! Yet somehow, from somewhere deep within, she wonders if there will be an answer to anyone's shouts. Where could all those people have gone?

At last, she stands alone on the sidewalk, her shoulders heaving, breathing hard. Her weary eyes come to rest on a Science Fiction coming attraction poster. Exhausted by her outburst of panic that sent her circling the parking lot in a frantic search for her friend, her Hollywood-influenced mind begins to develop several dramatic scenarios. She closes her eyes and presses her fingers to her temples in deep reflection.

She sighs, "Okay Amy, now just think about it for a minute. What happened to Heather tonight? Did she really just disappear? Where could she have gone? Why didn't I disappear? Am I insane?"

She imagines that Heather's disappearance might have happened while she was either looking down at her new shoes or looking at movie posters. She's quite sure she wasn't looking directly at Heather when it happened. In fact, it happened so quickly that now her mind is not able to fix on the exact sequence of events up to Heather's disappearance.

Amy allows her mind to entertain some worst-case scenarios. What if a professional abductor dressed in dark clothes down to his black tennis shoes had quickly and quietly snatched her from the sidewalk where they were walking? She squinted hard as she even tried to remember if there was either the sound of an approaching car, or a van speeding off while she was looking in another direction. Could she have been talking so loudly and not paid any attention at all to the sound of an approaching or departing vehicle?

Amy then rationalizes that possibly she could have been so distracted while obsessing over the great deal she got on her new shoes that she wouldn't have noticed Heather's actions or anything else! Maybe while she was looking down at those new Sketchers and talking her head off, Heather had gone into the theater, purchased their tickets, and had gotten in line for Coke and popcorn. And then she might have gotten lost in that crazy crowd running out of the theater!

Or, maybe Heather had left her pocketbook in the car and had gone back for it. "Yeah! That's it!" She shouts in relief as she snaps her fingers!

Amy's heart swells with hope for an instant as she tries to remember if Heather had her pocketbook with her on the sidewalk. After a tiny smile of hopeful anticipation, she scurries across the nearly empty parking lot toward her car.

"After all," she shouts, "people just don't disappear!"

As she nears the car, she strains her eyes hoping to see Heather's silhouette sitting there waiting for her with some explanation of why she abruptly ran back. Her heart sinks into her stomach again. No such luck! No Heather! Not even her pocketbook! Now she knows something unthinkable has happened to her friend.

She sits quietly in the car for a moment. She shakes her head slowly as she ventures yet more possible reasons for Heather's disappearance. The faint scent of her friend's favorite perfume convinces her of at least one fact...they did come to the theater that evening!

She is brought from her deep thoughts back to reality by the sound of horns blaring and brakes squealing as traffic on the main street by the parking lot is getting more and more out of control. In the distance the differing sounds of police sirens and emergency vehicles create an eerie, stereophonic cacophony as they wail and honk and scream from all directions. She feels like she is playing a minor role in a B grade disaster flick. In the midst of the howling din she turns the key and the motor responds. Without even thinking and as if driven by some inner 'need-to-know' Amy does something for the first time ever. She desperately turns her radio dial in search of an all-news station.

Quickly she finds an announcer who is attempting to maintain both his composure and his professional broadcaster's voice. However, the unmistakable tones of fear and panic emerge intermittently as he moves from one amazing report to another. Amy can almost picture the beads of sweat as they appear on this announcer's forehead and combine to form a steady flow, eventually dripping onto each news copy handed to him. The pitch of his voice rises with the level of incredibility as he relates the stories from all over the city and around the world.

"And (uh-um) listen to this!" he said, clearing his throat, "Similar reports are coming in from airports all over the world. Air traffic controllers are at a loss to explain simultaneous runway accidents and unexplained crashes. Their best explanation of what may have taken place is that either several of the on-board computer systems went out at approximately the same time, or that in many cases there were simply no pilots at the controls! In a related story, Police stations in literally every American city are swamped with 911 calls. Vehicles everywhere are reportedly crashing into each other. The causes for the crashes are neither speed nor weather related. On-the-scene eyewitnesses maintain their stories about dodging unmanned vehicles."

"And this...just in from the National Homeland Security Department...there is a high level of speculation that a massive terrorist plot has been launched throughout the United States. The plan, supposedly several years in developing, calls for the use of high-tech, radio-wave transmissions capable of taking over the computer system of any vehicle. That includes nearly all forms of transportation in America! Once the guidance system is taken over, all computerized functions can be manipulated by an external controller."

"And folks, you won't believe this one...Dr. Wayne Gordon, a specialist with NASA, has set up an emergency conference to consider the authenticity of recent deep space probes received and decoded. According to Dr. Gordon, there is undisputable scientific evidence that coded transmissions were being received from extra-terrestrial alien intelligence for over a decade. He is just one among several renowned scientists who have been pushing the Pentagon to study the possibilities of preparation for intergalactic warfare. With the sudden unexplained disappearance of several key military personnel, Gordon is convinced that alien abductions are the only feasible conclusion."

"Back on the local scene...well, the station manager here at KBBK has just confirmed what the staff has been speculating about for the past thirty minutes. He called all of the other stations in our area and, sure enough, all switchboards are lit up with calls from people who are reporting their friends and family members missing! All 911 emergency lines have, likewise, been jammed. It seems that the stories are just too much alike to be some kind of gigantic hoax! I don't mind telling you, folks. My intern from the seminary stepped out for a cup of coffee about thirty minutes ago and hasn't returned! Man! These stories are starting to get to me! Uh oh! Hold on folks! It's my wife on my cell phone...I've got to take this call...

WHAT? Well where did he go? Oh my God! Okay, okay, I'll be right there! Sorry, folks but my son is missing...good luck and G-G-God help us..."

As the dead air hissed its annoying static, Amy switched to another station thinking that maybe good old KBBK was just pulling their usual prank on their listeners. Her mind settled on that *War of the Worlds* program that sent the nation into panic decades earlier. To her horror the same bewildering stories were being related on each station. Her eyes danced nervously as she tuned in to the local Christian station. She thought that surely the truth would be told by Christians! The silence she heard was *deafening!*

She seethed through clenched teeth, "Why aren't the Christians talking about this mess? Why aren't they even playing their music? Wait a minute. Maybe they've moved to another call number. Oh, well." She sank dejectedly down into her bucket seat.

Frustrated and weary, Amy decided to drive home. As she drove she couldn't stop thinking about why she had even tuned to a Christian station. Amy had only been to church a few times with some of her Christian friends. Strangely, in the midst of all that was happening, she couldn't even remember their names. She could, however, remember that there was always something different about them. It wasn't just socially related either. The Christians she knew seemed somehow fearless. They seemed to have an inner strength. They weren't as easily frazzled by life's little problems as she and her friends were. Why couldn't she remember just one of them? If she could, she thought she might call one of them and maybe get a different perspective on what was happening. Just then it hit her like a slap in the face.

"Hey!" She perked up. "Heather is a Christian!" Amy knew now that if she could just find Heather, all of her questions might be answered. Where could she have gone? How could she leave so quickly and without a word to her best friend? Whatever Heather's reason, it must have been something pretty important. She had always been a very reliable friend. Just then Amy remembered something. It was Heather who had insistently dragged her kicking and screaming to church a time or two! But, try as she would, Amy just couldn't remember anything about the circumstances under which she went to Heather's church. She couldn't remember anything that was said or sung or prayed. She only remembered two things. She went because Heather had broken down her resistance, and it was the most boring experience next to going out with Chad Berringer, the preacher's son!

Amy suddenly realized something as she sat in yet another traffic jam. Though she was surrounded by the sounds of police and emergency vehicle sirens, thoughts of Heather seemed to dominate her focus. She settled into her bucket seat and exhaled a long, controlled sigh. Intuitively she felt that she would never see Heather again. As a scrapbook of childhood memories of the two of them paraded through her mind, she knew that she was closing the chapter of her life entitled "Heather." The most amazing thing about it was the fact that her sense of loss was now being replaced by concern for herself and her place in the midst of the terror and panic around her. At that moment try as she would, she could not be moved by the apparent loss of her best friend.

What had happened to Heather? What had happened to Amy? What will happen to the whole world? These questions can only be answered by the Word of God. The Bible has prepared believers for the rapture of the church. Heather was a believer in Jesus Christ. Both her life and her life style were yielded to the Master and Creator of the universe. Therefore, as an adopted member of God's eternal family, her departure from the realm of the earth marked her entry into the eternal realm of heaven. Her earthly body was instantly changed into a body like the resurrected body of Jesus. Her instant transformation at the rapture was for the purpose of inhabiting heaven and the new earth that God will create.

Amy had been in the presence of Christians. She had observed their worship of and their service to their God. She had met and rejected the Light of the Gospel in favor of her own selfish desires. When Heather was around her, the Holy Spirit had witnessed to Amy through the goodness and godliness of her Christian friend. At any time she could have accepted the light. All the times she had seen Heather choose right over wrong had been perceived as nothing more to her than something nerdy and laughable. Likewise, the times she had seen Heather pray over her meals simply amused and irritated her.

The kindness Heather had shown toward her enemies, the absence of profanity in her speech, the joy that was ever present in her life; all these lifestyle testimonies had meant nothing to Amy. However, one thing about Heather's absence will forever have a profound effect on Amy. When Heather was raptured out of the realm of the earth, the Holy Spirit of God went with her and all the other departed Christians. Heather's absence marks the absence of the Holy Spirit from this planet for a bleak period of seven years.

Amy's life and lifestyle will remain the same for a while. As the months pass, however, she will become even more egocentric. She will begin to think mainly of her own needs and desires. Soon the whole world will come under the control of a super dictator with whom she totally agrees. She will be among the first to eagerly receive the digital implant in her hand that insures her ability to work and live in the new world order of the Antichrist (Revelation 13:16-17). She will wildly cheer his ascension to world domination. She will agree with his plan to annihilate the nation of Israel. She will also work to assist him in hunting down not only Jews, but every person that refuses to worship him as God. Her life on earth will end in a plague caused by a nuclear holocaust near the end of the seven years of tribulation. Her afterlife will be one of eternal suffering in a place created by God for Satan, his fallen angels, and all humans who have rejected the grace and mercy of the Lord Jesus.

CHAPTER TWELVE

RELIGION AFTER THE RAPTURE

The world will be a different place without the restraining power of the Holy Spirit. The presence of the Holy Spirit in the lives of believers accomplishes something for the whole world. He keeps evil within definite parameters. Even as evil as the deeds of men may seem, the restraining power of the Holy Spirit within Christians keeps the lid on Pandora's Box. When the restraining force is removed, the restraining lid will likewise be removed. The holy boundaries now enforced on the powers of darkness will be removed. There will literally be no boundaries for evil in this world. Though evil men certainly strive to rule during this present age, they shall encounter no deterrence after the rapture. Godly moral conscience will have vacated leaving behind an environment where human life has no value other than as pawns for evil masters. Humanity will jump on the fast track toward absolute tyranny.

Secular Humanism will become the accepted world-wide religion. The code of conduct for the day will be 'every man for himself.' Of course, for a few years Judaism,

Islam, Catholicism, and New Age systems will remain on the scene as if nothing has happened. Likewise, under the umbrella of Secular Humanism, the usual suspects will practice their deceptive schemes. These include the Eastern Mystic groups, the Prosperity Denominations, The Pseudo-Christian Denominations and the Satanic Cults. Although many Denominations will still call themselves Christian, they will continue to believe in a Jesus who is very different from the One who has taken His Church out of the world and into heaven.

The Prosperity Denominations are those who claim that faith in Jesus brings health, wealth and profitable positioning. They also say that Jesus died so that *they may live* eternally. Even if this sounds like true Christian doctrine, they translate the meaning of the phrase *they may live* to mean that they may have their glorious heavenly afterlife as well as a financially secure and blest existence now! They suppose that Jesus was wounded so that their non-Christian-service related wounds could be healed. This is a perversion of the Scripture verse *with His stripes we are healed* (Isaiah 53:5). The verse applies to our salvation and not to our accidents and illnesses.

Prosperity religion preaches that when Jesus said He would prepare for *them* a mansion (John 14:2), He meant that they would live *on earth* in a mansion. They say that they not only will get a home in the *sweet by and by*, but that they also get their piece of the pie in a *suite here and now*. They rationalize that Jesus was poor so that they could be made financially wealthy. It is plain to see that without the Holy Spirit they can not accept the concept of eternal life in heaven that is promised to those who are persecuted for righteousness' sake on earth (Matthew 5:10).

The rewards for those of the prosperity preaching persuasion are not in heaven but exclusively on earth. Jesus said that we must lay up for ourselves treasures in heaven; for where our treasure is, there our hearts will be also (Matthew 6:19-20). The treasures Jesus spoke of are the souls of those who are converted as a result of our sharing the Gospel with them. The prosperity types have their sites set on earthly riches, comforts, and benefits. They do not understand the things of the Spirit for their desires are on the comforts of the flesh. If God honors their greed and selfishness, He will owe a tremendous apology to those who starved and died for the sake of the Gospel. The term *hunger and thirst for righteousness sake* (Matthew 5:6) has no appeal for a prosperity person. Their appetites are for wealth and influence on earth.

The term *Pseudo-Christian Denomination* applies to two types of religious organizations. The easiest one to tag is the group that wears the name of Jesus Christ but clearly embraces a belief in a Jesus that is not found in the Scriptures. The best illustration is found in the Church of Jesus Christ of Latter Day Saints (Mormons). The Jesus they believe in is not found in the Holy Scriptures. Although they use the King James Version of the Bible, they maintain that Jesus is not God. That claim alone disqualifies them from being Christian. They believe that Jesus is the spirit-brother of Lucifer (who became Satan). To put it simply, any organization that denies the full deity of Jesus, specifically that Jesus is also God, is not a Christian organization. Neither do Mormons believe in hell as a physical place of eternal damnation and punishment for those who reject the Gospel.

Another type of pseudo-Christian denomination is relatively hard to pin down. They call themselves Non-Denominationalists. This creates a complicated approach to pseudo-Christianity. Try to imagine groups of people with conflicting ideas about Jesus, yet, attempting to worship Jesus together! Which Jesus are they worshipping when they worship together? They are so ignorant about the Biblical concept of a unified belief system that they actually call themselves a non-denominational denomination! Their attempt is well-intended but anti-Scriptural. The Scripture points to dwelling together in unity (Psalm 133:1), not in ambiguity!

Usually the members of non-denominational churches are only unified by their extreme dislike of and contempt for mainline denominations! The groups consist largely of people who have been scarred by unpleasant experiences in one or more of the mainline denominational groups. For emotional refuge they have sought out a place *"Where everybody just loves Jesus!"* Of course, heaven is the only place in existence where that is true. While on earth those folks are doomed to continue their search on a regular basis! It's called *church hopping!*

Since a great percentage of members in any church is most likely unregenerate, there is NO PERFECT CHURCH ORGANIZATION on earth. The Great Commission stands opposed to such psychological nonsense as a non-denominational church. Jesus commissioned and empowered His church to go into all the world and make disciples (Matthew 28:19). He said that we must preach the unified (one and only) Gospel. He never said His church would be a bunch of non-confrontational friends who just agree to disagree concerning church doctrines! We must remember that the Word of God exhorts the children of God to dwell together in unity. A church that allows many contradictory views among its membership essentially stands for nothing and normally doesn't stand for very long! The real question is, "How could so many people in so many denominations say they believe the Bible, but still be confused about who Jesus is?"

Likewise, how could so many intelligent people not know that the rapture is God's way of announcing the end of the Age of Grace for the Gentiles? When the book of Revelation refers to the return of Jesus, the scenario involves Jesus setting up a thousand year reign on earth (Revelation 20:6). At His return He will have believers from all the ages with Him in glorified bodies. How could this occur unless at some point in time previous to His return He also raptures the church out of the earth? It is to this question that post-tribbers say Jesus will only appear at His second coming after the Great Tribulation. That way, those who endure to the end of the tribulation will be saved. They believe that only then the dead in Christ will rise, the true believers will be changed and caught up in the air with them and the returning Christ, and they will all begin the thousand-year reign with no perceivable absence from the earth.

The afore-mentioned scenario sounds logical, but what about the removal of the restraining force that Paul wrote about? The only way the antichrist will be able to gain psychic control of the minds of the world's people is in the absence of the Holy Spirit who now serves as a restraining force against the man of lawlessness (2 Thessalonians 2:7). Therefore, how can believers remain when the Holy Spirit is removed? If the Holy Spirit is taken out of the world, He would also then be taken out of believers! Therefore, the rapture is the event whereby God will remove the Holy Spirit and all believers from the earth. Those who remain on the earth will do so apart from any possible influence of the Holy Spirit. People will be left to the mind-control of the antichrist, who will have no problem securing his place as absolute world leader in the absence of any kind of holiness. The earth will truly become a world without a godly moral conscience.

This brings us to the last religious group that will be practicing on the earth during the Tribulation. Satanic Cults are groups that religiously worship and serve Satan. One of the most recognizable names among satanic cult leaders is Anton LaVey, the founder of the Church of Satan. Among his followers and disciples are confessed mass-murderers Charles Manson, Marilyn Manson, and Richard Ramirez.

LaVey and his co-founder Kenneth Anger admitted to duping many into following their cultic practices. They deceptively pedaled their ideas as not being about the dark prince, the devil. Satanism has spread rapidly as simply the worship of the Light God. We must remember that the Bible says that Satan can appear as an *angel of light* (2 Corinthians 11:14). By soft-selling the religious practice as a type of New Age mysticism, the leaders of Satanic Cults are able to get people to renounce Jesus and the God of Scriptures for "another way" to heaven. Some even see it as another method of worshipping Mother Earth!

Of course, hard core Satanists practice the black arts in conjuring spirits and casting death curses upon those who would destroy their covens. These works could hardly be expected to win someone a resting place of eternal peace! Actually, the lie that has been told promises to the most ardent followers a place of honor with Satan in hell. In order to swallow this kind of line, the parishioners must be convinced that hell is NOT what the Bible describes it as; a place of eternal, fiery torment.

There should be no doubt that God's Word strictly forbids all of the practices of Satanism. Revelation 22:15 lists the practices that will keep people out of God's eternal kingdom. They include sorcery, sexual immorality, murder, idolatry, and lying deceptions (Revelation 22:15). All of these practices are included as part of the Satanic Church creed. Can there be any doubt that the Church of Satan will still be meeting after the rapture?

CHAPTER THIRTEEN

THE REIGN OF THE ANTICHRIST

For forty-two months after the rapture the Antichrist will enjoy the favor of the earth's people and an exalted position as world leader. Satan will send him a demonic helper that the Bible calls *the beast* (Revelation 13:11-15). They will be assisted by signs and wonders accomplished through Satan's empowerment. There will be no Holy Spirit-empowered gift of discernment on earth whereby the Antichrist might be seen for who he is. He will have complete success in his deception of the nations (2 Thessalonians 2:9-11). No one will oppose his system of world government. All of the operating systems of the world will belong completely to Satan and his pawns for seven years!

However, at the mid-point of the seven years the Antichrist will stand in the temple in Jerusalem and announce to the world that he is actually none other than God Almighty! Because of his impressive miracles, all but one group of people will believe his claim and worship him. That group is the Jews. It should be noted that the Jews will not be convinced by the then-absent

Holy Spirit. They will rely on their comprehension of the Law and the Prophets. The Old Testament account of Messiah's coming is completely different from the way by which the Antichrist will have come to power. Therefore, the Jews will not accept his self-proclamation as their God. Following their rejection of him as God, things will take a dreadful turn for Israel. They will be severely persecuted from that point until the spectacular return of Jesus forty-two months later.

The final forty-two months of the Great Tribulation will see the rage of the Antichrist and all the other nations poured out on the Jews. The covenant people of God will see worse persecution than ever before in history. The term *Great Tribulation* will refer not only to the violent treatment of the earth, but also to the horrible treatment afforded all of those who reject the Antichrist. During this persecution some Jews will join together in an attempt to turn people to the true God. They will try to expose the Antichrist with the message that the true God will soon be sending His Messiah for the salvation of the Jews, His covenant people.

Notice that this author believes that the Jews are STILL God's covenant people! There are some silly Protestants and Catholics who have been deceived into believing that God has revoked Israel's status as the chosen children of God. This is not, nor can it ever be the case. What God has promised cannot be broken. The grass may wither and the leaf may fade, but the Word of God stands forever!

Some believe that these are the 144,000 Jewish evangelists spoken of in Revelation 14:1-4. These Jews have not worshiped the beast, but have faithfully looked for the coming of Messiah. As forth-tellers of the coming of the Messiah, they technically qualify as evangelists, though they do not embrace the Gospel message. They will believe that this is the (first) coming of Messiah for which they have long awaited. They will not know until Messiah comes that He is the Lord Jesus. They will not know that Jesus is their Messiah until they look upon Him whom their forefathers crucified!

During the final stages of the Tribulation God will also raise up two evangelists who will openly defy the Antichrist. They will declare that he is not God, but that God is coming to judge the earth (Revelation 11:3-12). These two will have power from God to perform mighty miracles to enhance their preparation for the coming of Messiah. After they have prophesied for a while, they will be mocked by the Antichrist and murdered. Their bodies will be publicly displayed for three and a half days in Jerusalem. After those days, they will come to life as a sign from God that they have told the truth. The two witnesses will be taken up into heaven before the on-looking eyes of the whole world. The Antichrist will then call for the obliteration of Israel. He will orchestrate a final battle to achieve his threat concerning their annihilation.

With the preparation of the Antichrist for war against God's people there will also come an answer from heaven. A number of visits to the earth by angels will see terrible calamities poured out in series upon all who have accepted the mark of the beast (Revelation 14 6:18). The first three angels serve as messengers to the people on earth. They will glorify God and then warn of the fury that will befall those who worship the beast and have received the mark. After those three, the Lord

Jesus from heaven will begin to harvest the earth. After Him, three other angels will visit further calamities upon those on earth. Indeed, great tribulation will transpire on the earth!

Finally, the Antichrist will amass his armies for the final assault on Jerusalem. The armies of the Antichrist will be made of soldiers from many nations including 200 million from the Middle East and the Orient. They will meet outside of Jerusalem on a field called Megiddo for what the Bible refers to as the Battle of Armageddon. It is a battle that will not even involve Jewish participation.

Just as the armies of the Antichrist attack the Jews, the Lord Jesus, the Word of God, will gloriously burst into this realm accompanied by His Church and His angels. He will be riding a white horse, and on His thigh will be the name KING OF KINGS AND LORD OF LORDS (Revelation 19:13-16)! His rout of the enemies of Israel will be so complete that the blood of the enemy will flow at a depth of five feet. All of the combative enemies of Israel will be destroyed. The Antichrist, the beast, and Satan will be bound in a pit for the duration of Christ's thousand-year reign on earth. The return of Jesus and His Church will occur at the end of the seven years of the world's Great Tribulation.

The millennial reign of Jesus with His Church is not a difficult concept to grasp. Both Jesus and His believers who return with Him will have eternal, spiritual bodies. Those who are still alive on the earth will have earthly, human bodies. Earth will be governed during the millennial reign by Jesus and His returning believers. Though it is impossible to know how those with eternal, spiritual bodies will rule over the earth, one could speculate in this manner: We know that the resurrected Jesus could eat food, disappear and reappear, go through solid matter, disguise His appearance, and more than likely exercise all of the miraculous powers He displayed while on the earth. The Apostle John said that when He appears, we shall be like Him (1 John 3:2).

If we are like Him according to the Scriptures, dare I suggest that we will be endowed with some or all of His abilities? Will we who return with Jesus be equipped with powers for the judging of nations and angels and the ruling of the people of earth for a thousand years? We know that the earth will still have a population of three to four billion people because one-third will be destroyed during the course of the Tribulation. The people who remain will have seen the return of Jesus because the Scriptures say that every eye shall behold Him when He comes. Will we have cities or counties or districts to judge and evangelize during the thousand years? Enough speculating! Let's go on to Paul's assertions concerning the rapture.

CHAPTER FOURTEEN

THE APOSTLE'S PROOF

Today there are many great theologians with nearly as many differing interpretations of Scripture concerning the Rapture of the Church. Interpretations range from no rapture at all to rapture which coincides with the second coming of Jesus at the end of the Tribulation just prior to the millennial reign. Of all the interpretations of various Scripture passages, I choose the Holy Spirit-inspired writings of Paul, the great missionary and Apostle. Certainly we should be able to accept the teachings of a man credited with authoring nearly half of the books of the New Testament!

Compared to the deeper teachings of Paul, his doctrine of the rapture is quite simple. In fact, its simplicity is what may have caused Nineteenth and Twentieth Century theologians a bit of a problem. Because the mantra of those times called for a preponderance of thick, weighty ideals related to the higher intellectual criticism of Bible concepts, those critics may have actually lost their grasp of the true nature of the Gospel.

Namely, "Whosoever shall not receive the kingdom of God as a little child, he shall in no wise enter therein" (Luke 18:17).

Paul wrote an instructional letter to the church of the Thessalonians concerning their fear that their relatives who were Christians and had passed away might miss the return of Jesus (1 Thessalonians 4:13-18). He comforted them with the truth from the Holy Spirit. What he told them is applicable to the church today. He wrote that those believers who are living at the reappearing of the Lord will not precede those who have passed away in the faith. He then gave them what I believe to be the basic doctrine of The Rapture of the Church.

Paul wrote that Jesus would descend from heaven with a shout, and the dead in Christ will rise. Those who are alive at that time will be caught up together with the resurrected ones in the clouds to meet the Lord in the air. That "catching up" is what is referred to as the Rapture of the Church! Paul maintained that this teaching was *by the word of the Lord.* Those who teach any other Gospel than this are threatened by Paul with the curse of God!

Paul also related prophesy about the cultural climate of the Day of the Lord (1 Thessalonians 5:1-4). In verse nine of that chapter the Apostle sums up our escape from the coming Tribulation. He states that God did not appoint believers to wrath, but to obtain salvation through the Lord, Jesus Christ. Within the context of what Paul had been addressing, I understand this to mean that believers will be taken out of the world at the rapture prior to the outpouring of God's wrath on those who refused to accept His Son, Jesus. A clearer statement would be that God never intended for those who choose

Jesus over the world to be exposed to the world's final time of Tribulation.

What kinds of tribulation will the earth experience? The Bible records seven bowls of wrath poured out *on the earth* (Revelation 16:2-21). The punishments are as follows:

1. Boils appear on those who worship the Beast.
2. The oceans become as dead men's blood, killing all ocean creatures.
3. The fresh waters become blood.
4. Men are scorched by heat from the sun.
5. The kingdom of the beast becomes darkened, and his followers are in pain. Because of the pain and the sores, they continue to curse God!
6. The Euphrates River is dried up to prepare a dry highway for the kings of the east who will march on Jerusalem. Demons are sent out by Satan to gather them together for Armageddon.
7. The whole earth is utterly shaken by an earthquake that divides Jerusalem into three parts and causes the cities of the nations to fall. Every island sinks and the mountains fall. Hundred-pound hailstones fall on the people.

After reading about the Tribulation wrath, one can see why God did not assign believers to such a time.

The people in Thessalonica to whom Paul had written, however, would not have known about John's account in the Revelation since it wasn't written for another forty-five years. Apparently there arose some dispute over Paul's statements in his first letter to that church. His second letter seems to be a more precise explanation of the events surrounding the reappearing of Jesus. The church is apparently experiencing serious persecution at the time of Paul's second letter. So much so that Paul congratulates them for their patience and faith amidst persecution (Chapter 1:4). They were suffering for their faith in Jesus. In light of this Paul writes to them a word of consolation that remains for us a hint concerning rapture doctrine.

In verse six Paul relates that it is the righteousness of God that will repay the persecutors of believers with tribulation. Although the word tribulation is not capitalized in this verse, we may accept the teaching, combined with verse nine of chapter five in the first letter, that we are not appointed to suffer the wrath of God that will be poured out on the unrighteous during their time of tribulation. Again in verse seven, Paul states that the Thessalonians (and we who believe) will be given rest with him when Jesus is revealed. This clearly indicates that believers will be spared the flaming fires of wrath in the Tribulation, having been raptured to be with the Lord.

In Chapter two of his second letter Paul writes a few lines of clarification. Apparently there had arisen some false teaching concerning the rapture of the church. Some of the believers were worried that the day had already come and they had missed Jesus' reappearing. Paul assures them in verses three and four that because the man of lawlessness had not yet appeared, the day could not have come! Simply put, this means that the rapture could not yet have happened. The order of things, according to Paul was as follows: First, the rapture would occur; then (because of the absence of the Holy Spirit) the man of lawlessness would appear, exalt himself, and eventually claim to be God.

Paul explains the absence of the Holy Spirit (He who restrains the powers of evil) in verses six and seven. This is a clear teaching that the Holy Spirit will be taken out of the way at the Rapture of the Church, so that the lawless one can be revealed. (Remember that the Holy Spirit indwells all believers so that as we leave, He also leaves!) At that point the Antichrist will be revealed according to the working of Satan with all power, signs, and lying wonders with which he will deceive the world. The world will then consist of all who have not chosen the love of the truth (Verse 10). The deceived world will consist of those who did not believe the truth but had pleasure in unrighteousness (verses 11 & 12).

Believe it or not there are those who deny that the rapture will occur before the Great Tribulation. They even use these same verses of Scripture to support their claim that the rapture will occur after the Great Tribulation! My request is that the reader would take into consideration the goal of the Word of God. It is to be used as a lamp to shine the light of the Gospel to the entire world. Anything that poses a threat to that ministry or stands as a hindrance to the Great Commission of the Lord can not be considered the will of the God of the Word! Given the imminent return of Jesus, and the fact that after His reappearing and our rapture no one can be saved during the Tribulation, it seems right to share the Word of God now, and with great urgency and enthusiasm! Let's face it. There will be no second chance for Gentiles to receive Jesus after the rapture and during the Great Tribulation. For this reason let us with all haste and fervor share the Gospel with everyone, everywhere until He comes. The Lord says, "Today is the day of salvation!"

CHAPTER FIFTEEN

A MASTER DECEIVER

It seems that the church members who could care less about the rapture are also those who are very comfortable in the little, socially oriented, religious clubs they call a church. They are so comfortable that they don't really want the church to be raptured. The very thought of it makes their skin crawl. They not only make no attempt to understand it, they are repulsed and even offended by the idea of their non-religious friends being left behind! Their ideals concerning holiness and righteousness have been so compromised by their desire to be friends with the world that they would rather accept any other doctrines than those grounded in God's truth.

When the rapture occurs, how will these so-called Christian denominations rationalize the absence of the true believers? By what forms of deception will they be deluded by the master deceiver? At that point in the world's history the playing field will have been leveled. The chief adversary will literally have no opposition. The Holy Spirit and all believers will have been removed from this realm by the Rapture of the Church.

Because Satan knows the Word of God better than anyone on earth, I wonder if he looks forward to the rapture almost as much as believers do. Once the convicting power of the Holy Spirit is out of the way, he will enjoy true sovereignty over all the people on earth. With the close of the Age of Grace all gentiles will have made their final choice to either accept Jesus or reject Him. Those who have rejected Jesus will have either purposefully or inadvertently accepted the lordship of Satan. That day for which Satan impatiently awaits will finally come.

As mentioned before the Bible declares that the Antichrist will rise to power with the aid of miraculous signs, convincing the hearts of the world that he is their true ruler. No doubt he will be able to satisfactorily explain away the rapture to the masses. Unlike Jesus, whose supernatural works raised the suspicious eyebrows of the religious authorities, the miracles of the Antichrist will gain the whole-hearted acceptance of the world. All nations will submit to his dominion. Without the guiding influence of the Holy Spirit, the world will easily be convinced that this new charismatic leader might even be a god!

The Antichrist will not be a god. He is nothing more than a man permitted by God to be used by Satan to deceive the nations that have rejected Jesus. God will send them a delusion (2 Thessalonians 2:11). The Antichrist will lead the nations down the primrose path of perceived glory with three and a half years of seeming global prosperity. Satan's number one strategy for gaining followers will not have changed over the millennia. He will still employ the deceptive formula of "follow me and my miracles and you will forever be prosperous." His main advantage during the Age of Grace has been the fact that men will usually accept that which they can see, hear, smell, touch and even eat over the promises of an unseen God. In the Antichrist people will have the advantage of experiencing what they believe to be a god in their very presence.

The turning point in the glory ride will occur when the Antichrist announces that he is God Almighty. His outrageous self-coronation will occur three and a half years into the Tribulation. At that point it will be clear to the Jews that Satan is the puppet master of this great world leader. Their wake-up call will be the fact that he will use the newly rebuilt Temple in Jerusalem as his new throne. This may be acceptable for the rest of the world, but it will be pure blasphemy to the Jews. They crucified Jesus for claiming to be God. For once their dogmatic adherence to the Torah will serve them well. According to their Old Testament Scriptures, the Messiah will come on a white horse to begin His reign over all the earth. They know that the Messiah will come from the sky. They believe the Messiah will place Israel over all the nations.

Israel's refusal to acknowledge the Antichrist as God will place Israel at the top of every nation's hate-list. It will literally divide the world into two camps — Israel and everyone else! It will also drive the Antichrist to require allegiance to him as a prerequisite for living. He will set up the global enforcement of allegiance to his lordship. People will either submit to his rule or face strict economic sanctions, including death! It will literally be his way or the highway to nowhere! To ensure worldwide compliance, a universal system of accounting will be put into force. Purchase of food and other necessities will be permitted under strict guidelines. Everyone will be required to display their world-government-supplied identification numbers in order to make any purchase.

The Antichrist will not only possess miraculous abilities, but also great intellect. To avoid the possibility of being defrauded, he will require that identification numbers be attached to the bodies of all people. The Bible calls the identification process the *mark of the beast* (Revelation 13:16-17). Before the 21st Century, there was no other time in world history when the technology for such a marking was possible. Today it is possible to place an informational microchip no larger that the head of a pin under the skin. The data on the chips can be easily checked for verification by global informational computer systems. Such a chip can also be used in conjunction with satellite tracking devices to pinpoint the whereabouts of its host.

The Bible speaks of an identifying mark on the forehead or the hand. If an accounting microchip was buried within the cranium, its placement or removal by someone other than a surgeon could result in serious brain damage or death. Likewise, if the chip were implanted near vital arteries or nerves in the hand, its removal by an amateur might result in great blood loss, crippling, or even death. Regardless of the life threatening effects in either case, the host would pay with his life for such an offense against the Antichrist. It would be very simple to track down a removed chip. Once discovered after removal, the process of finding the host would be "no problemo."

But why would anyone want to remove the chip that was so much more than just their meal ticket? It was also their link to their god, the Antichrist. Having accepted him as their god and provider, why would they denounce him and refuse his provision? Apart from any allegiance to the Antichrist, why would people choose to give up their only means of social survival? Thousands today continue their employment in the service of awful companies and employers that they loathe. They stick with their jobs strictly for the pay and the benefits they receive without any real sense of loyalty to the company.

There will only be two types of people on earth during the seven years following the rapture: those who accept the Antichrist's mark and those who don't. Those who don't accept the mark might further be divided into those who resist for religious (not spiritual) reasons and those who live in communal farming villages.

Communal farming groups may see no need to take the mark. Since it would not enhance their economic position, they may decide to opt out. These groups consist of people in many areas of the world who have subsisted entirely without any dependence upon the industrialized societies. Because they and their ancestry have learned to utilize the earth's bounty, they have known no other lifestyle. They are entirely self-sufficient concerning what they eat and wear. They are skillful at living off of the land. The Antichrist may not try to disciple them because they have neither wealth nor a perceivable purpose in his grand scheme of global dominion.

Pseudo-Christians may also refrain from taking the mark because they might actually believe that Jesus is coming to rescue them soon. They missed the rapture because they had an errant view of Jesus. Because their view is errant, they are still looking for Him to return and either rapture them out or set up His reign in lieu of the rapture. They are reminiscent of the Jewish leaders who saw Jesus. Those teachers of the Law and the Prophets had an errant view concerning the coming of the Messiah. They were so self-deceived that they missed the first coming of Jesus altogether (Romans 10:3). Because of their self-righteousness, they couldn't recognize God in the flesh!

Another religious group that will resist taking the mark is the Jews. After the Antichrist announces that he is God, the Jews will distance themselves from him in an attempt to remain holy. They will recognize his blatant blasphemy and have nothing to do with his world system. There is a large enough community of Jewish-based industries to provide support for Jews who refuse the mark. Of course the Antichrist will bring his power to bear on all who attempt to deal with the Jews. It will end up being the world against the Jews. It is because of God's covenant relationship with them that they will see Him when He comes to save them at Armageddon.

CHAPTER SIXTEEN

TRIBULATION SALVATION?

Recently many authors have written novels concerning post-rapture events. Some have deliriously engaged in romanticizing their works by suggesting that Gentiles will be saved after the rapture. Such a concept fails to take into consideration the necessary work of the Holy Spirit in the regeneration of a soul. The refusal to believe that Jesus both instituted and will close an Age of Grace for the Gentiles is a grave error with serious consequences. There are many reasons why Gentiles can not be saved after the rapture and during the time of the Great Tribulation.

According to the Apostle Paul it was always God's plan that during the past two thousand years the Gospel would be made available to every person on earth. Paul was under the impression that it was the Jews' rejection of Jesus as the Lamb of God that led to the Gentiles having an opportunity to receive the Gospel (Romans 11:25). However, our omniscient God foreknew that Jesus would be rejected by the Jews and would then commission His disciples to take the Gospel to the whole world. The truth is that God has always loved all people and that adoption into God's family was His master plan from the beginning. We must suppose that, had Israel received Jesus as the Messiah when He came, they would have been commissioned to evangelize the rest of the world.

Paul wrote to the church in Rome about how the spread of the Gospel had been redirected to the Gentiles due to Israel's general rejection of Jesus as the Messiah. Because of their murderous rejection of Jesus, God placed the Jerusalem Jews in the regrettable position of never being able to understand that Messiah had come. This was a fulfillment of Old Testament prophesies (Deuteronomy 29:4 & Isaiah 29:10). Subsequently, because of their rejection of Jesus, they were blinded to the truth about Him so that they could not believe and be saved.

The glorious truth is that from before the foundation of the earth, God intended for all nations to come to an understanding of His great love for men. Mankind had inherited Adam's fallen position as sinners unable to redeem themselves (Romans 5:12-14). Jesus' blood is the necessary payment for the redemption of the sins of all people. God *chose* the Jewish nation as the vessel through which Jesus, the promised Savior in God's covenant with Adam, would come. Jesus said that He was sent to the Jews first, and then for all people. In other words, the *chosen* Jewish nation held a special place in the heart of God since they would provide His Son's ancestry. John the Apostle wrote that Jesus came unto His own, and His own rejected Him (John 1:11)!

In recent Centuries as Christianity has enjoyed relative popularity most Jews have been content to consider Jesus as simply a great prophet and master teacher. They also know that He was crucified because He claimed to be the Son of God. This brings up some serious questions. If Jewish law states that anyone who is hanged on a tree (crucified) is cursed, how could that jive with their current claim that Jesus was also a great prophet? And the fact that Jesus' own teachings held Him to be the Messiah of God, likewise, flies in the face of their approval of Him as a master teacher! Could a liar also be a master teacher? Could a cursed criminal also be a great prophet? Because of these overwhelming inconsistencies in their beliefs about Jesus, most Jews will not accept Him as the Messiah. That is, until they see Him riding into Jerusalem on a white stallion as their Conquering King!

Just try to comprehend these two amazing reactions of people everywhere. First of all, in spite of the similar, life-changing testimonies of millions of believers over two millennia, most people today deny the reality of Jesus' life, death, and resurrection. Secondly, and even more amazing is the fact that non-believing church members who are left behind after the rapture still won't be able to accept that the rapture is a Biblical reality!

The reasons behind these two positions are actually generational in nature. It is true that many people will not accept the Gospel because they reject the Christian lifestyle. In fact, even most church members tend to avoid the disciplines of the faith. The younger folks would rather eat, drink, and be merry while they can enjoy their youthfulness. The older folks would rather hold on to their weekend habits or enjoy their retirement travel plans than be actively involved in the local church ministry. The idea of being labeled a *holy Joe* does not appeal to the young. Working in the local church is too time-consuming for post-retirement schedules. It isn't so much about holiness or love for the Savior as it is about lifestyles and convenience!

After the rapture, unsaved people will not be able to understand what has happened to the believers. They will be *in the dark* because of the absence of the Holy Spirit whose function is to enlighten minds in the areas of spiritual truth. It is precisely that area of spiritual truth that escapes the great majority of church members today concerning anything spiritual. Because these church members are not believers, they do not have the Holy Spirit to guide them in areas of spiritual truth. Therefore, they are not only susceptible, but eager to receive every wind of false doctrine and non-spiritual speculation.

A common misconception is that once non-Christians witness the rapture of their friends or family members, they will immediately confess, repent, and believe! This belief is fostered by an overflow of human emotions rather than spiritual enlightenment by the Holy Spirit. Certainly, anyone who witnesses the rapture before their very eyes would be foolish to deny the supernatural event. Furthermore, having seen it, they would have to believe it! Unfortunately, the point is not even arguable. But, the problem is two-fold.

The first problem has to do with the exercise of our faith. For two millennia Christians have believed in Jesus. Their belief was not as a result of having *seen* Him, but rather, because of their Holy Spirit-based faith that the Word of God is true.

Jesus said that His disciple, Thomas, was blessed because he *saw* the resurrected Lord and believed. Then Jesus said that those who believed in His resurrection *without seeing* Him would be even more blessed (John 20:29)! The declaration of Thomas that Jesus was his Lord and his God did not require as much faith as it does for someone like you or me who have never seen Jesus and yet believe! Faith comes by hearing and believing the Word of God.

Before His ascension, Jesus commissioned His disciples (and all successive believers) to share the truth of the love of God with all people everywhere. People were expected to respond to the truth based on the faithful witness of those who had seen Jesus! They would never actually see Jesus with earthly eyes, but they were called on to believe the report of the Holy Spirit-empowered witnesses. Millions have surrendered their lives to the Lordship of Jesus based solely upon the witness of other believers. Although no believers today have ever *seen* the Lord, their *faith* in Him is rewarded with salvation from sin and the reality of eternal life.

Concerning Christianity, if you have to see something in order to believe it, where is the element of faith? The truth is that if you have to see Jesus to believe in Him, you'll never see Him! It is only by (God's) grace that we are saved through (our own) faith in Jesus. Because we believe the Word, God rewards our faith with salvation. Faith is the *exercise* of our belief in Jesus. As we exercise our faith, God gifts us with more faith to trust Him even more each day. The greatest reward is when He gives us more ministries to do in His name. Our faith is the ever-increasing gift of God that enables us to obey Jesus' commands even though we have never seen Him on the earth. Neither do we ever see all of the results of our personal ministries. Nevertheless, we must faithfully execute all of His commands.

The second problem for those left behind is intangible. Because the convicting, convincing, and sealing power of the Holy Spirit will no longer be available to Gentiles after the rapture, how will anyone be able to exercise faith unto salvation? Even if they have witnessed the rapture, the most they can hope for is a gnawing, emotional realization that their Christian friend or family member might have been telling the truth. People may even feel sorrow over their rejection of Jesus. They may feel distraught that they missed the rapture. They most likely will be like the demons who, as James has written, believe that Jesus is who the Word says that He is, and tremble in fear of His power without accepting His Lordship. People may believe, but they will not have access to the faith that enables them to obey Jesus' commands. The powers of darkness will eventually overwhelm them to the point that they are driven into deep depression, but without godly repentance.

Today there are many deeply depressed people in America. The field of Psychiatric Counseling is expanding exponentially. Perhaps you know someone who knows exactly what they must do to improve their physical or emotional condition, but just can't seem to act on their counselor's prescribed behaviors. Likewise, associates or family members of raptured Christians may possibly spend time ruing their bad decisions. However, they can never experience the convicting, life-changing power of the Holy Spirit who has departed from the earth. They may even suspect the truth, but they will not be able to experience a holy desire to obey the Word of God. Eventually, with the passing of time their minds will engage their defense mechanisms, and they will forget about their losses. They will settle into the regular humdrum routines that will define their lives until the Antichrist takes control of their world.

CHAPTER SEVENTEEN

THE CHURCH OF SOCIAL REFORM

B ut what about those lost people who have been church members for decades? Some of the most highly regarded theologians of this Century estimate that lost church members currently make up between seventy-five and ninety percent of most mainline denominational congregations. Their estimations, considered to be judgmental by some, are based on several reliable social indicators. These indicators provide insight into what passes for a church in this century. At a time when telling the truth is optional if it requires a change of lifestyle, many are willing to turn a blind eye and a deaf ear to the self-indulgent sin that runs rampant in mainstream denominational churches.

One of the saddest misnomers currently circulating in religious circles is the term *evangelical*. The word should hint at the spread of the Gospel of Jesus Christ. In fact, Webster's Dictionary gives its first definition as: *of, relating to, or being in agreement with the Christian gospel especially as it is presented in the four Gospels.* Jesus commissioned all Christians to the task of global *evangelization.* Evangelizing the world involves the process of telling the story of God's love for all people. The story begins with Jesus and ends with Jesus. The contents of the Gospel are all about Jesus and His obedient life, His sacrificial death, His prophesied burial, and His glorious resurrection. The story climaxes with the forgiveness of sin available to all people who believe. The conclusion of the Gospel is that Jesus is God in the flesh! The application of the Gospel is that there is salvation in no one else but Jesus of Nazareth, the Lamb of God, who is the risen Lord of all creation.

To label an individual as an evangelical minister or a member of an evangelical church or denomination is to acknowledge that he or she is all about spreading, preaching, and teaching the Gospel of Jesus Christ for the conversion of the lost and the discipling of converts. If a person is spreading or teaching something other than the Gospel, they are not an evangelical anything. In contrast, the thing they may be spreading is a counterfeit Gospel known as the *Social Gospel.* The Social Gospel is formulated on the concept that Jesus came so that people could enjoy life's social amenities while experiencing God's favor here on earth. The Social Gospel is rooted in the perception that people might be more easily persuaded to believe in Jesus if they are first provided better living conditions. The Social Gospel is not the Gospel of Jesus Christ. Therefore, it is a lie out of hell! It cannot save anyone from hell! And yet today it is the primary message of most mainline denominations!

The ministers of the Social Gospel are vastly popular and widely accepted as *evangelical* ministers. They write wonderful, best-selling books about how to live a better life and how to get along with everybody, including members of anti-Christian religions! Scriptures are quoted out of context to suggest that worldly success is the result of godly living and social concern. There are even books based on the lie that if you can be the friend of the world and call yourself a Christian, people might one day accept your type of Christianity. However, if they do, they will be damned by your false doctrines and your disobedience to the Word of God.

Of course the Social Gospel is exactly what Satan wants everyone to believe! He perverts the Word so that people think that "*love your neighbor*" means to be tolerant toward anti-Christian religions and reluctant to speak the truth lest you seem confrontational! The Scriptures, however, reveal that a friend of the world is an enemy with God (James 4:4). Christians are to consider themselves aliens and strangers (1 Peter 2:11) in the world. They are to be *in* the world but not *of* the world. Being socially and politically correct should never be confused with being spiritually sound. The world hates Jesus! Therefore, His believers can never embrace the world's ideals.

Should the church not address the issues of poverty and disenfranchisement? Should these areas be left to government agencies or volunteer humanitarian agencies? Jesus said that His primary mission was to seek and to save that which was lost. What was lost? We know that man's relationship with God took a huge hit in the Garden of Eden. We know that Jesus came to restore mankind to the Father. Feeding five thousand men miraculously was definitely a great miracle, but it was not the reason Jesus came. The miraculous feedings and other miracles were intended as illustrations of both the mercy and the creative power of Jesus as God in the flesh. He came to show mankind that God Himself was willing to come to earth on a love-mission to restore a broken relationship with His beloved creation.

There are many reasons why the Social Gospel is a good example of apostasy. For the sake of socialization mainline denominational churches are permitting increasing numbers of practicing homosexuals to hold church membership. Catholic and Anglican Bishops are being busted regularly as pedophiles. As bad as these problems are, many church members and many ministers maintain that membership of homosexuals in any church should not even *be* a problem! In fact, the mention of this practice by a Twenty-First Century author probably won't raise a fraction as many eyebrows as it would have in the 1950's. The sad truth is that media coverage of hundreds of cases of homosexuality, child molestation, and general immorality among high ranking members of the clergy in the Catholic and Episcopalian Churches has paved the way for blasé acceptance of this abominable trend.

Let not the reader be confused as to this author's position concerning the practice of homosexuality. It is, was, and ever shall be an abomination in the eyes of our Holy, Almighty God (1 Corinthians 6:9)! On this concept the Holy Scriptures are abundantly clear to all who fear the Lord! Jesus came neither to diminish nor abolish any principle concerning

God's order. This includes the mandates referring to procreation, the instructions concerning marriage, and the restrictions and corrective actions pertaining to immoral practices. A person that practices homosexuality whether through personal involvement or in agreement as to its legitimacy stands against God and in danger of His judgment. Some great theologian once said that if America isn't punished for embracing homosexuality as an accepted lifestyle, God owes Sodom and Gomorrah an apology!

Notice that I went right to the most blatant violation of God's moral code. Homosexuality is the sin that mocks God's design for the propagation of mankind. It is also an attack on His institution of marriage. To suggest that a government recognize same-sex couples as being legally married is to place homosexuality on an even plain with the normal, God-ordained institution of marriage.

Homosexuality is the manifestation of the wickedness that brought about the destruction of Sodom and Gomorrah (Genesis 19:24 & 25) and other ungodly, ancient civilizations. Lust for one's own gender is an acquired desire. Any practicing or self-styled psychologist or psychiatrist who accuses God of mistakenly placing in an individual a sexual desire for his or her own gender not only commits blasphemy; he or she becomes both a social and spiritual stumbling block. Such social and emotional confusion comes only from Satan, the inventor of deception.

Because God is holy, by definition He is incapable of lying. When He created Adam and Eve as male and female, He set the prototypes for all men and women, including their sexual orientation. Only a fool would dismiss God as a fumbling creator who mixes up the genders at birth. Of course all suggestions that demean the personage and wisdom of Almighty God are designed to enhance Satan's assault on marriage, the family, and ultimately, the kingdom of God.

Check out Satan's mindset. In order to convince the American people that an activity referred to as an *abomination* in God's Word should be acceptable; he goes to work on an obvious inroad to our mainstream, societal minds. He uses the movies, television sit-coms, foreign cultural influences, and other high impact media saturation to show that homosexual people are really nice folks…often even humanitarian and philanthropic!

Rest assured that homosexuality did not spring full blown onto the American church scene. Rather, it is the logical result of the ever-weakening position of American churches concerning sin. One only need recall the account of Ananias and Sapphira in the New Testament. Their lie was so repugnant to the Holy Spirit that they died on the spot when confronted by Peter (Acts 5:1-10). You must believe that the New Testament church's holiness factor increased greatly following their funerals! The early church loved the Lord in that they reverenced His holy nature with lifestyles that reflected it. It should be noted that the early church enjoyed accelerated growth in the light of her surrendered obedience to the holy commands of their holy Lord Jesus. May it be so today!

CHAPTER EIGHTEEN

THE UNREPENTANT CHURCH

B oth Jesus and the Apostle Paul gave careful instructions as to how sin must be handled in the church. If a person is caught in sin, those who are spiritually mature are charged with restoring him or her (Galatians 6:1). Here is much of the problem in Twenty-First Century churches. There apparently is so much sin among church members, it is nearly impossible to find those who would be considered *spiritually mature* enough for such a spiritual confrontation! Also, the level of *pseudo-piety* is so great that most individuals are afraid to act as one who is spiritually mature for fear of being labeled a holy Joe!

Some fear that, should they attempt to spiritually counsel a brother who is sinning, some of their own sins will be brought into the open for all to see. Another weakness comes from ignorance of the Scriptures. Many will say that they do not confront others because *we're not supposed to judge!* How are we to help those in sin with our godly counsel if we're not supposed to judge whether or not they are even sinning? Let's face it! Most people today are more content thinking that the sins of others are none of their business! The Lord, however, knows that sin in any form keeps the church from carrying out its mission of global evangelism.

Sin is a terrible problem not only for individual church members but for the entire congregation. The Apostle Paul depicted the church as being one body having many members (1 Corinthians 12:27). For the church to function properly it takes the inter-connecting of everyone's spiritual gift. Likewise, the sins of individual members affect the holiness of the entire body.

To think that one's private sin is a personal matter points to a gross misunderstanding of the Scriptures regarding the body of Christ. Sin renders the spiritual power and authority of a church ineffective. Therefore, when the sin is discovered, it must be dealt with for the health and the effectiveness of the body of Christ. Confession and restoration are the Biblical mandates for dealing with sin in the church. Where sin is the problem; restoration is the ultimate goal.

Jesus outlined the steps toward restoration (Matthew 18:15-17). First, the person is approached discretely and made aware that his or her sin is known. If there is no repentance, several believers are to confront the person so that a valid witness can be established. If the person still will not repent, he or she is to be brought before the entire congregation and asked to repent. If the person refuses to turn from his or her sin, he or she is to be excluded from fellowship with other believers until repentance is accomplished.

The purpose for this procedure is so that the church, by being obedient to the commands of Jesus, will be found holy and blameless as His bride at His coming. The primary importance of maintaining a holy character is to insure that the church enjoys the power of the Holy Spirit in the accomplishment of its mission of global evangelism. Woe to that minister and all other believers who do nothing about known sin in the congregation!

Another indicator of sin in the church is broken marriages. In America over one half of *all* the marriages which began in recent decades have ended in divorce. The percentage of divorces among church members is nearly equal to that of the unchurched public. Since it is safe to assume that marriage break-ups are the result of sin, it must also be concluded that there are many church members who find marriage to be something other than a spiritual union and a sacred institution. In other words, there is a lot of messing around going on inside the church these days! There are many cases where couples in a church will divorce, stay in the same church, and marry other members within that church!

The worst-case scenario in a church is when the preacher is caught having had immoral relationships with a number of the women in his congregation. In one church where this occurred, the congregation did nothing more than prescribe professional counseling for the preacher. They even paid for the sessions! Deacons have run off with preachers' wives. Music Ministers have run off with accompanists. Teenagers have been impregnated by Youth Ministers. What if all of this has happened within the same congregation over a period of thirty years! With pastors, staff members, and deacons providing sinful examples, how could one expect to grow a spiritually healthy congregation? How could one believe that the Spirit of the Lord would lend His power in the midst of such unrestrained sinfulness?

One may ask, "Isn't there forgiveness for divorce?" We must all admit that with forgiveness there is freedom from sin. However, there is no freedom from the earthly consequences of sin. The Word of God is true. People will always reap what they sow! Jesus said that divorce for any reason other than adultery is a compounding sin. If a man divorces a woman for any reason other than adultery, and that woman remarries, the first husband is the cause of her ongoing adultery with her second husband. His sin is compounded daily and is classified as a lifestyle of sin, especially if he marries another woman. In that case he also will be living in adultery. What about the woman? Literally, the woman is not to remarry unless her first husband dies! Until that time the church becomes her point of refuge with God as her spiritual head.

If there were only a few divorces each year within the church, one might simply deduce that those involved were not able to forgive completely the way that Jesus forgives. However, the fact that the occurrence of divorce is so out of control suggests that many couples never really understand the high regard placed on the marriage covenant by the Word of God.

The constant stream of ungodly occurrences indicates the level of gross sin within local churches in America. Sin is the primary reason churches suffer from ineffective ministries and a lack of spiritual influence in their communities. The pure and unified church is designed to be the separate and holy body of the Lord. Our primary purpose is to witness the love of God to all people. As salt and light, the church is supposed to be the most positive of all influences in the world. However, as the time of the rapture draws near, the church is becoming more and more like the world! No wonder Jesus asked the rhetorical question, "Nevertheless, when the Son of Man comes, will He really find faith on the earth?" (Luke 18:8)

Teenage pregnancy among church members is at the same level as that of unchurched teens. So much for rearing children in the fear and admonition of the Lord! Here is a simple formula: if churched children are raised like unchurched children, they will act and react like unchurched children! What about the households where both parents work and have little or no time to disciple their children? Does the family really need all of the little extras a double salary can buy? Or does the family really need the blessing of the Lord for remaining true to the Scriptural command to raise children in the fear and admonition of the Lord? Do you think one or two hours of attending church youth programming each week can have the same influence as several hours of MTV, R-rated movies, X-rated internet, and hanging out with the unchurched gang?

Another sin problem with both spiritual and cultural effects is that of having children out of wedlock. This takes place on a daily basis in America. And yet our government honors such behavior with a financial welfare benefit. Although this abuse of Federal funding is seen in poverty level households across racial lines, the most flagrant abuse is among Afro-Americans.

It has been reported that 70% of Afro-American babies born in 2007 were born to un-wed mothers. In many families Federal money for childcare support is the only source of income.

We have Federal laws for the protection of the infants, but what about God's laws? Young women are having babies without a husband! The Bible calls sex before marriage the immoral act of fornication! It is a clear case of governmental enablement! It should also be considered illegal! Isn't making money by committing immoral acts considered prostitution? Many of the illegitimate babies are born to girls in Middle School. In many cases the young mother either doesn't know or will not say who the father is, so she can't get anyone to support the baby financially. The government then provides financial support for the unwed mother and her child. The young mother soon figures out the more bastard children she gives birth to, the more government money she will be paid. Therefore, the government is paying these women and girls to have sex and birth babies! Does that make sense to you?

The real problem in the preceding paragraph is the acceptance of sexual promiscuity as a cultural norm within the Afro-American community. In 1991 a would-be black rap artist explained the male-female relationship regarding sexual activity to this author. The man was talking about all of the different women he had slept with that week. His banter begged the question concerning how this was possible, seeing that he was a member of a local church. He was very happy to explain the facts. He said that because Eve caused Adam to sin, from that moment forward, all women were under the dominion of all men. He explained that women were incapable of refusing sex to men. I asked him if any woman had ever refused him. He smiled and said, "Well, maybe a few might have!" I then asked him where he received that brand of theology. He said that all black preachers preach it from their pulpits! I could only hope that this young man was just making up his own theology. I believe that it is as irresponsible not to preach the truth about sexual promiscuity as it is to preach in favor of it!

Gambling, drinking, lying, cheating, stealing, coveting, sexual fantasizing and other sins play major roles in the life-styles of many adult church members of all denominations. A typical reaction comes in the favorite Methodist phrase *all things in moderation*. The Bible phrase *be holy as your Father in Heaven is holy* has fallen from realism into the category of idealism. When faced with hard-core sin issues within the church, lost church members employ Biblical ignorance as they cry out, "Well, I don't want to be judgmental!" This misunderstanding of Scripture needs to be cleared up once and for all! The church IS SUPPOSED TO JUDGE! We are to bear in mind that our disposition in judging, whether righteous or unrighteous, is the way we will be judged!

The non-confrontational approach of never calling out sinners is widespread among today's church leadership. This pseudo-leadership style has paved the way for a type of church that *has the appearance of godliness, but denies the power of the Holy Spirit!* When the rapture occurs, clergymen and church members like these will not be taken up. What do you suppose their reactions will be?

CHAPTER NINETEEN

STORY II: THE LOST CHURCH MEMBER

The following scenario is one way to depict what will happen to those who have been members of a church fellowship but have never known Jesus as their Lord. Let's use a very common situation found in many church families in America. We will look at a typical Baptist family of four in the southeastern part of the country. The reader need not be offended if this scenario hits close to home. Rather, if the shoe fits, you might consider making a decision that will change the tragic outcome of this short story for you.

Ted is a great guy. He has been very successful in the operation of his own company. He has owned and operated a Christian Bookstore in a small southern town for the past ten years. Ted has a wonderful family which includes Claire, his wife, and their two beautiful children. Ted Junior is nine and Missy is seven. They are all members of the First Baptist Church in their town. Ted is a deacon and Claire sings in the choir.

Claire is the daughter of a Southern Baptist pastor. While growing up she traveled extensively with her parents who served in several churches throughout the Southern United States. Claire accepted Jesus as Savior and Lord and was baptized at the age of seven. Since that time she has lived a meaningful life of service for the Lord. When she was young, she often imagined marrying a preacher and raising a family like the one in which she was reared. Besides serving in the choir, Claire attends every adult Bible study and women's mission study she can. She is an outstanding witness and participates in the weekly outreach ministry of her church. As a Sunday School teacher she has led many young girls to faith in Jesus. Claire helps Ted at his store as often as she can. She has also led people to Christ while helping them find Bibles and other items at the bookstore.

Ted Junior received Jesus as Savior and Lord at the age of eight. He loves his church and attends Sunday School and the AWANA program, a combined Bible training and recreational ministry. He has also experienced some persecution at the public school for defending his faith. He told his mom that he shouldn't get so upset. After all, look what they did to Jesus! He is learning to pray for those who mistreat him because he is a Christian. He gets most of his encouragement from his mom. Whenever he approaches his dad on the subject, Ted smiles and sends him to Claire. He uses phrases like, "You better speak with your mother about things like that," or "Son, now that's right up your mom's alley!" Because of his great admiration and respect for his father, Junior thinks nothing of it when his dad refers him to his mom concerning spiritual issues. Junior is still too young to pick up on the fact that his dad really doesn't have a handle on what the Bible says concerning the problems that might confront an eight-year old believer.

Missy has begun to really watch her mother. She has noticed that her mother prays at the family meal. She knows that it is her mom who insistently gets everyone ready for Sunday School each Sunday morning. She especially admires the joyful attitude that her mom exudes in every thing she does. Claire is quickly becoming Missy's hero. Missy wants to be just like her mom! She wants to have both the energy and the influence that her mom has. She wonders how her mom got the way she is. She has not yet concluded that her mom's actions and reactions are based on a personal relationship with Jesus.

One Sunday Missy saw her brother go forward at the conclusion of a church service. Two weeks later she was present at his baptism. She saw how pleased her mom was with the whole thing. Her understanding of what had happened to her brother could be summed up by her inner thoughts. "If I go forward and get baptized, maybe mom will make a big fuss over me, too!" Obviously, Missy did not yet understand what giving one's heart to Jesus entails. However, Claire noticed her daughter's interest and began to spend extra time during the Bible stories at tuck-in time each night.

Ted believes that he is a Christian. He and several other young boys went forward together on Youth Night during a spring revival meeting twenty-five years ago. All of the boys attended the same Sunday School class and were in the

Royal Ambassador group together. They had grown up in the church and had followed the annual tradition of youth night at revival. Their names were proudly added to the recorded salvation experiences. Their fathers, uncles and grandfathers had all basically followed the same tradition. The boys were all baptized together in a creek that ran beside the church cemetery. Ted and his friends were eleven or twelve years old. None of their lives changed to any noticeable degree. They were still as rambunctious as most boys their age. And, like most boys their age, they did not have a personal relationship with Jesus Christ.

Ted met Claire while they were attending the local community college. Ted was a typical nearly-alcoholic fraternity brother. He loved Claire's purity and straight forwardness. He was impressed by her spiritual depth. He knew that she would be the kind of mother he wanted for his future children. Contrary to the counsel of her parents, Claire saw in Ted a challenge for reforming. She was sure that she could change him into a fine Christian man who would make a solid, godly example for her future children.

Alas, Ted never really changed. However, because he followed Claire's lead in attending church regularly, he was eventually seen as deacon material. The fact that he had a successful business (out of which Claire gave a tenth to the church) helped in paving the way for him to be considered for the deacon board. Sure enough when he turned twenty-five, he was nominated to serve as deacon and was elected to serve by the church membership. The leadership would have made him a deacon sooner, but the church by-laws stated that a man must be at least twenty-five years of age.

Ted still had not changed. He continued to hit the bottle in secret whenever he was worried about his business. He used less-than-ethical practices when figuring his taxes. He talked Claire into allowing the HBO and SHOWTIME cable television channels into their home. He watched the sleazy adult programs and movies after Claire and the kids went to sleep. He did not attend his children's' school events, and he gladly deferred all of their spiritual training to their mom and their Sunday School teachers. Ted was a cheat, a liar, a pervert, and worst of all, a horrible example for his children. Though he was completely immune to Bible teaching and preaching, Ted put on his Sunday suit and played the church game wearing his smiley-face mask every week.

It happened on a beautiful Sunday morning. Ted woke up after getting to sleep well after midnight. He rose slowly and fixed his gaze on the alarm clock. The large LED indicator said 9:26. Ted pondered for a moment whether it was Saturday or Sunday. When he settled his mind that it was Sunday, he hit the floor anxiously.

He ran to his closet thinking, "Well, she finally did it!" Claire had been having difficulty getting Ted out of bed on Sundays for some time. She had even threatened to just leave him in bed and take the kids to church by herself.

"Yep! She finally did it," he grumbled as he struggled into his suit pants. "Now I'm gonna be late for the early deacons' meeting. What the #@*!* was she thinking?"

As Ted sat fuming on the side of the bed fumbling with his shoe strings he noticed something very strange. Claire usually laid out her clothes, shoes, and matching handbag on various pieces of bedroom furniture every Saturday night so she could get a jump on the usual herding of the children through their hectic Sunday morning routine. What Ted saw froze him in his tracks. All of Claire's clothes were there; neatly in place awaiting her rising.

"Wait a minute! Something's very wrong here," Ted thought as he made his way to the children's rooms. He stood in the doorway of Junior's room not sure of what he hoped he'd find. He knew that Junior's clothes were always laid out for him. His heart nearly stopped as he saw a set of Sunday pants folded neatly on a chair and his son's dress shirt draped on the chair back. Junior's shoes and socks were underneath the chair.

He thought to himself, "They haven't left yet! Why haven't they left yet? Where is everybody?"

Ted raced down the stairs toward the kitchen shouting, "Claire! Kids! What's going on? Are we staying home today?"

What he found in the kitchen stabbed him once more in the chest. There were neither the signs nor smells of breakfast, nor was there any hint of disturbance. The kitchen was in its usual perfect condition. Ted plopped down heavily in a chair and stared at the breakfast table. His mind seemed to be stuck in an indefinable mode. At the same time that Ted was wondering where his family was, he was also thinking that he would miss his deacons' meeting and what the other deacons might think of him. He finally concluded that he should simply get up, get dressed, and go to the church. As an afterthought he decided that Claire and the kids had probably just gotten up late, picked out different clothes to wear, and rushed off to the church. He smiled and shook his head thinking how stupidly he had been acting.

Ted was in such a hurry when he got into his car, he didn't even notice that Claire's car was exactly where it was the night before. He was half-way to church when he realized that her car was still in the garage when he left.

"She must've ridden with the Smiths," he thought. "What's wrong with that #@!!%# Honda this time?"

When Ted arrived at his usual parking place at the church, he noticed that several of the church staff parking spaces were still empty.

"At least I'm not the only one late today!" he thought, chuckling to himself. He had been so focused on getting to his usual parking space he had not noticed that a large number of the usual cars were also absent. Though he had rushed to the door, he paused as if something had gripped him. He slowly turned, scanning the usually crowded parking lot. He had not seen so many cars missing since the peak summer vacation time. Shrugging it off as the result of some flu epidemic, he charged down the hall to the deacons' conference room.

The church had twenty-nine active deacons who met monthly to pray and discuss ministry needs. On this day, however, only fifteen had made the meeting. Ted entered the conference room only to find an ambience of low mumbling voices coming from deeply concerned faces.

Looking up, the chairman announced, "Look! It's Ted!" Several of the deacons rose and headed in his direction. Their faces expressed a mixture of both delight and confusion.

Bill Danforth quickly asked, "Ted, have you heard from John or David or Wes or..."

"Hold on Bill!" Ted said as he grabbed Bill's shoulders. "Settle down and tell me what's going on in here!" "Where the...um, where are the other deacons?"

A strange silence engulfed the group of bewildered men. Nervous eyes searched questioning countenances until finally Fred, the chairman, spoke.

"Well men, I guess we need to go on with our meeting. I know we've never had this many deacons to miss our conference without calling in, but we need to go on anyway."

Ted suggested, "Fred, shouldn't we try to call the others? I'm not sure what's going on, but Claire and the kids weren't home when I got up today, and their Sunday school clothes were all laid out. Either they came on in without getting me up or ... look, I don't know if there's even a connection, but I just feel like we need to try and contact these other men."

As Ted was relating his story about Claire and the kids, he noticed how some of the men seemed to be sinking into a state of deep depression. Many of them muttered phrases like, "O my God" and "Dear Jesus," and some mumbled the names of their loved ones. For some reason no one wanted to outwardly voice their fears as to what might have happened to their own wives and children. His words had a confirming effect on many of the men present. Others remained in complete and defiant denial. Fred staggered to his feet.

After searching the long faces of the deacons, he sighed deeply, cleared his throat and said, "Maybe Ted has the right idea. I recommend…" Just then he caught himself mid-sentence. He realized that he was trying to maintain the lofty position of chairman of the deacons at a time when open honesty should prevail.

He cleared his throat again. "C'mon men," he began with a softer tone, "let's go to the office and get on all available phone lines in an attempt to contact our brother deacons. We've just got to find out for certain if what we all are thinking is true."

Fred's words served as a wake up call to Ted. As if startled out of a deep slumber he rose quickly and asked, "What do mean by what we all are thinking?"

Ted's eyes darted back and forth at the men on either side of him. "Hey," he shouted, "What exactly are you guys thinking? Somebody please say something!"

A sense of paranoia began to sink into Ted's heart. He truly had no idea what Fred and some of the others were so concerned about.

"Well," he bristled, "I'm going to the office like Fred suggested. Bill! Dave! C'mon, let's go do some calling!"

As the four men made their way to the office they heard mixed sounds of sobs and mumbling coming from many of the Sunday School classrooms they passed. As deacons they had the impulse to stop and see if they were needed, but their mission to call the other deacons propelled them forward to the office phones.

Suddenly their mission was interrupted by a loud shriek! They stopped in their tracks as Elsie Haynes, an elderly woman from the Adult Seven Hannah Class, approached them as rapidly as her seventy-nine-year-old frame would allow.

"You must come quickly," she bleated, "Dear Mrs. Howell has fainted dead away. Poor thing! She's lying on our classroom floor! Come on, men! Please hurry!"

Perspiring heavily Fred said, "You men see if you can help Mrs. Howell. I'll get started with the phoning!"

As Fred ambled on toward the office the three other men accompanied Elsie to the aid of Mrs. Howell. The classroom was just around the corner. The men entered the room only to find Nora Jones kneeling over Mrs. Howell. Bill knew that Nora was a retired nurse.

"How's she doing, Miss Nora?" Bill asked as he patted her on the shoulder.

"Well, Bill," Nora responded, "I think she'll be alright. My guess is she just fainted. We all thought it might be her heart, you know, since she had all that trouble last spring; but I think she's just worked herself into a tizzy and passed out!"

"What in the world brought all this on, Miss Nora?" Ted broke in, "What were you ladies discussing today?"

"Well it all started when Myra there cracked a silly joke about why so many of our regulars were out today," Nora responded dryly. "It is strange that half of our ladies didn't make it in today. Myra said that it looks like the rapture must have taken place last night. Well, that got everybody all nervous to the point that several of our ladies said they noticed many cars missing from our parking lot. Betty Ann Myers even said her daughter didn't call her this morning for the first time in nearly twelve years. As the voices got louder and more people began talking all at once, poor Mrs. Howell began coughing and muttering, *"Oh no! Oh no!"* Then she fell over face-first onto the floor… bless her poor heart!"

"Brother Ted, you don't think the rapture has occurred, do you?" The question came from Annie Black in her sickly, nearly inaudible voice. "I tried to call my grandson, Billy, this morning to wish him happy birthday, but no one answered. The phone just kept on ringing and ringing! I told him I'd call him this morning. Where do you suppose he went? Was he raptured, Brother Ted? Why weren't we all raptured if Billy was?"

This was the first time Ted had allowed himself to even consider the possibility of the rapture even existing. He had never been convinced that the rapture was even a remote possibility. He had heard Claire speaking about it with some in one of her Bible Study groups, but as to its possibility, he just couldn't believe something like that was even a reality.

"No Miss Annie, I don't think Billy was raptured," Ted said in his rehearsed-deacon tone of voice. "You all shouldn't allow yourselves to get so worked up over a thing like the rapture," He continued. "Why, if there really was rapture, and if it had taken place, we would all have been raptured together…now wouldn't we? Everyone in our church would've been raptured! Now isn't that right, Miss Annie? Isn't that right, Brother Bill… Brother Dave?" Ted tried to bring the other deacons into the mix to reassure not only the ladies, but himself as well.

The other two men looked first at each other and then into the hopeful and expectant eyes around the room. When they offered no verbal support for his theory, Ted experienced a strange, sinking sensation. A growing sense of anger and frustration welled up in him because of the expectations of those surrounding him. There was also a tinge of fear as to the remote possibility that the rapture was not only a Biblical truth, but that it may have something to do with the fact that he couldn't find his family that morning. His reaction, along with that of the two other deacons served to plunge the women of the Adult Seven Ladies Hannah Class into a state of bewildered melancholy. As he stared into the hollow, hopeless eyes of those ladies, Ted somehow suspected that he would never see his wonderful family again.

Just then the door flew open to reveal Fred. "No answer at any of the numbers I called!" Fred said in a hushed tone. He wasn't out of breath, but he sounded that way to keep from alarming the ladies. As he glanced from face to face Fred, too, began to experience the onset of depression. He knew that something terrible was wrong, but just what it was he was afraid to say.

"Now, everything will be alright, ladies," Fred finally said, "you all just go back to your lesson and we'll get back to our deacons meeting. C'mon men, let's go."

While the other men headed back to the conference room, Ted went to the Children's Department to find Claire and the kids. The Children's Department was in another building. There Ted found mostly empty classrooms that were usually bustling with the sounds of four and five year olds. Likewise the First and Second Grade classrooms were completely vacant, including Missy's room. Ted finally ran into a couple of ladies in the hall who were pondering the extremely low attendance.

He asked, "Have you seen my wife, Claire, this morning? She teaches Third Grade Girls."

"No," they replied, "We haven't seen any of the lower grade children or teachers this morning. Do you suppose they are all on a field trip or something? Why didn't we get the notice?" Obviously the two had no idea where Claire and Missy were. Troubled by the reaction of the two ladies, Ted ran from the building back to the Conference Room.

In a matter of minutes Ted and the other men seemed to recover from whatever gloom had momentarily beset them. Ted began to resign himself to the fact that, although he didn't really know where Claire and the kids had gone, he was sure there was some simple, logical explanation for their absence. Likewise, the other members of the church simply went back to their Sunday School lessons.

With the exception of a reference now and then to one of the missing class members, the class sessions continued almost as if nothing had interrupted them. The classes quickly resumed their debate on whether or not the Apostle Paul was the author of the epistle to the Hebrews or on some other topic of study.

Several weeks went by. Ted and many others within his social circle truly missed their loved ones. Many times their busy schedules were interrupted by thoughts of their missing family members. They also often wondered what had happened to a number of their former clients and associates. Most people gladly accepted the prevailing notion that there had been an alien abduction on a global scale. After all, this was the theory put forth by the new President and his hastily-assembled Cabinet members. He was Ted's kind of guy...a man of great charisma and influence.

Though from time to time Ted would think of his family, there was always his own pursuit of personal success that quickly crowded out any time for remorse or regret. Any thoughts of recovering those who had mysteriously disappeared were gradually moved to the farthest reaches of his mind as stored but non-essential data. Because those tender memories were a source of confusion mixed with emotional pain, they were gradually replaced with other memories of personal successes and gratifying relationships that served to build up his ego.

CHAPTER TWENTY

GOOD PEOPLE?

Have you ever heard someone refer to the members of his or her church as good people? Maybe it's a Southern-styled rating system, but I have heard the term used that way many times over 34 years of local church ministry. An older gent from Walnut Street Baptist Church must have said *Walnut people are good people* a hundred times during my eight years of service there. I wanted to tell him each time he said it that there's a big difference between *good people* and *good Christian people!* Maybe that's what he meant, but you'd never know it by the serious lack of Bible literacy in that place!

How could someone attend all the Sunday School classes, worship services and Bible Studies that a church has to offer and still end up missing the rapture? Does attending church make a person a good Christian? What makes a person a *good* person? It's amazing to see how liberal the modern mindset is concerning what makes up a good person these days. It has been said that a person's life is a mixture of everything ever done and everyone ever known by that person. It has also been said that at the end of one's life, if the good things he or she has done outweigh the bad things, a pleasant afterlife will follow, supposing that there is an afterlife! The truth is there definitely is life after this life! How many *good* people believe that those who live a good life and are always considerate of others will definitely go to heaven?

For your own research try asking someone whether or not he or she is a *good* person. The answer will most likely be, "Well, I've never committed murder, rape, or grand theft!" Most Biblically illiterate people conclude that those who can get through life without murdering, raping, or robbing anyone will surely go to heaven. An even greater indication of how people rate others will be gained if you ask, "Do you think

_____ (fill in the blank with the name of someone you have suspicions about) is a *good* person?" You'll be surprised at how some people will stretch their imaginations to come up with something non-condemnatory! After all, no one wants to be guilty of judging others!

At funeral services for great dignitaries the eulogy usually contains the words, "He (or she) was a person of tremendous moral character." Morality must be one of the qualifying characteristics of a good person. Others will commend the dearly departed to heaven based on the fact that he or she was loved by everyone! I guess if everyone loves you, you're definitely a good person! Moreover, if people were extremely devout in their particular religious persuasions, most Americans would agree that surely they were good enough to be heaven-bound. To certify the general consensus a recent animated flick affirmed that all good dogs go to heaven!

There is at least some vestige of truth in the idea that getting to heaven has something to do with one's lifestyle and treatment of others. Whether or not going to heaven is based on man's own personal merits can easily be discovered by consulting the One who created both mankind and heaven. The penetrating Word of God shines the light of truth on all of the lofty but hazy ideals of unregenerate mankind. Not only does lost humanity very comfortably assert its own personal qualifications in deciding the criteria for attaining eternal life, but there also exists as many different pictures of heaven as there are religious denominations! The number of books written on the subject of the afterlife and its various qualifications would fill a very large library.

While it is good that mankind is able to sense the possibility of an afterlife scenario, it is distressing to see how many people avoid the simple truths that are found in God's Word concerning eternal life. As to whether or not man is good enough to qualify for heaven, God's Word says quite emphatically that all people have sinned and, therefore, fall short of God's glorious goodness (Romans 3:23). The Bible contrasts man's goodness with God's goodness by saying that man's goodness is like filthy rags when compared to God's idea of goodness. Purely for shock value many preachers have more carefully defined *filthy rags* as soiled menstrual cloths! Jesus asked a rich young ruler why he had addressed the Master as *good* teacher. Jesus' follow-up remark was that only God could be considered truly good.

Man is only good by man's own standards. He is not, nor can he ever be mentally, emotionally, or physically good enough to attain heavenly citizenship. Heaven is for those who are without sin. Under the inspiration of God's Holy Spirit Paul wrote that the wages of sin is death (Romans 6:23). Death in this sense means eternal separation from God. With the exception of Jesus all humans are sinners. Therefore, it is impossible for any sinful human to go to heaven. At this point many would consider God to be a mean and unusually cruel creator who has created heaven only for Himself and His angels.

Though some religionists may try, God cannot be blamed for the sins of mankind. Mankind was created with the ability to choose to do either his own will or God's will. A man can opt for either his own righteousness or the righteousness of God in Christ. God's Word states that it is not His desire that anyone should perish (2 Peter 3:9). Rather, it is His desire that all should repent of their sins having come to a saving knowledge of the forgiveness that is available through the atoning work of Jesus on the cross. Because Jesus died a sacrificial death to pay for all of our sins, we were placed in the position to receive forgiveness for those sins. However, we must exercise our God-given ability to choose to accept God's forgiveness for our sins. When we accept God's forgiveness and choose to live under His Lordship, God endows us with the righteousness of Christ and eternal life in heaven.

Foreknowing that His created order of man would almost always choose sin over obedience, God mercifully formulated a plan whereby man's sins could be forgiven. The working out of God's grace toward mankind involved no simple formula. God's universal law of forgiveness requires a blood-offering so that sin will be covered from God's sight. For this special sacrifice God required:

1. The death of a perfectly sinless man,
2. who was willing to die for sinful men,
3. and was willing to be tortured though innocent of any crime,
4. and was God in the flesh!

As impossible as it is for a human to fulfill all of these requirements, we must never forget that with God all things are possible! Just like when He provided a sacrificial ram for Abraham, God provided the needed sacrificial Lamb for all of mankind. He showed His love for sinful mankind in this way; He gave His only begotten Son to fulfill all of the requirements for our forgiveness (Romans 5:8). Jesus was born of the Spirit of God and an innocent virgin. He had a truly earthly mother and a truly heavenly Father. This meant that Jesus was not born of the earthly, sinful seed of Adam but of the supernatural, spiritual seed of God. This means that as the Son of God, Jesus is God!

Having established that Jesus is God, we now move to the next requirement. Even though Jesus is God, He had to be willing to submit with remarkable humility to the reviling and persecution reserved for guilty sinners. And though innocent of all accusations, Jesus obediently submitted His flesh to be ripped and torn, His name to be slandered and cursed, and

His Holiness to be questioned and rejected by men. He was willing for His holiness to be revoked by God as the sins of all of humanity, both past and future, were laid upon Him (Isaiah 53:6). He literally *became* the sins of all sinners! The Bible says that *He was led as a lamb to the slaughter*, and that *He opened not His mouth* in protest (Isaiah 53:7).

Jesus knew that while He existed in human form, He was capable both of suffering and giving up His life. Though He is referred to as the Light of the World, He was capable of being swallowed in the darkness of death. He knew that His willingness to suffer death for the sins of the world meant that He would be forsaken and separated from the Father. Jesus became our sins and was buried for three days. We must remember that for God a day is like a thousand years and vice-versa! For Jesus a day apart from the Father must have loomed in His mind as an eternity of time. Nonetheless, Jesus was willing to die for sinful mankind so that our sins could be forgiven. His death satisfied all of the requirements of the Law of God that stated *without the shedding of blood, there is no remission of sin* (Hebrews 9:22). Had Jesus not given His sinless life for sinful man there would be no possible way to receive forgiveness for our sins.

Some theologians mistakenly criticize the notion that people must ask for Jesus' forgiveness for their sins, since Jesus has already died for that very purpose. This criticism is used to establish the elitist approach of certain denominations. Such erroneous theology goes on to state that humans do not even possess the capability to ask for forgiveness apart from God's enablement. Reformed theologians also maintain that

God has pre-selected certain people to receive some kind of special grace that is neither intended for nor available to all people, but is reserved for a privileged few. This thinking is Satan's best ploy to date in his attempt to convince people that God is a prejudicial hater of most of mankind. They really believe that God hates everybody but them!

The truth is that God was reconciling all of the sons of Adam to Himself by sacrificing His Son, Jesus, in their place. Therefore, Jesus has paid the price for everyone's sins. God made a promise to Adam in the Garden of Eden after Adam had sinned. All who hear and accept the grace of God which was poured out on the world through the suffering, death, and resurrection of Jesus, will receive His forgiveness and eternal life. Our sins are removed through confession of the sufficiency of the blood of Jesus, the sacrificial Lamb of God. After such a confession and subsequent profession of faith in Jesus as Lord, people receive eternal life with God.

We must remember that it is our sin that makes communion with God impossible. Sin separates man from his Holy Creator. At a great cost God has offered mankind the blood of Jesus Christ, His only begotten Son, for the forgiveness of sin. Those who confess their sins, repent by directing their lives away from sin, and submit to the Lordship of Jesus will receive eternal life. Those who reject God's gracious offer of forgiveness and die in their sins condemn themselves to an eternity apart from God in a place of eternal torment intended for Satan and all of the fallen angels.

Surely one can see that a supreme Creator who would offer the life of His only Son as payment for the sins of mankind must be an exceedingly good and loving being. Add to this the fact that such a being would sacrifice His only Son with the foreknowledge that most of mankind would still reject His gracious offer of eternal life. God knew all along that most people would reject Jesus, choosing instead their own nonexistent goodness with the false hope of acquiring peace in their own imagined afterlife. Such a loving, giving individual as God must be considered more than merely special. No doubt all the combined good exercised by all of humankind throughout history can never measure up to the self-sacrificial goodness of the Lord God Almighty, the Creator of all things! Only God can be considered truly *good.* Can any other good thing done by mankind be compared to the Lord God's goodness in the free offer of His only Son? Certainly not! God and God alone is good!

There are many church members who profess to be good people. They also believe they are church members in good standing. Of course, they insist that they are also good Christian people. However, these church members have never witnessed to anyone about Jesus, have never gone out of their way to encourage anyone to seek God, have never given sacrificially, have never prayed in public, have never testified in the church or out of the church, have never served with others on a church committee, and have never had a personal devotional time in their life. They also believe they will be raptured when Jesus appears! What do you believe about yourself?

CHAPTER TWENTY-ONE

A HOLY SPIRIT-LESS WORLD

The previous chapter was written to prepare the reader for the logic needed to consider what the world will be like without the influence of the Holy Spirit of God. The Spirit of God will be removed from the earth. This will occur at the rapture of those who have accepted God's salvation through the forgiveness of their sins and have made Jesus the Lord of their lives. After the rapture the world will be a very different place. Gone will be those hearts that are guided by God's Holy Spirit. Gone will be the tender concern and compassion for the eternal souls of all men. Gone will be the spirit of sacrificial giving without regard to what might be received. Gone will be the Spirit that throughout the Age of Grace has been a restraining force designed to keep the god of this world, the adversary of both God and man, from completely perverting the hearts of all mankind. Most importantly, gone will be the Spirit of God that assists man's spirit in communing with God.

The Spirit of God provides the force necessary for the quickening, or bringing to life, of man's spirit. Prior to being influenced by the Holy Spirit, the spirit within a man is dead in trespasses and sins. Because it is completely preoccupied with self-gratification, man's unregenerate spirit constantly rebels against the Spirit of God (Romans 7:5-6). The unregenerate man is ruled by his mental and emotional impulses (Romans 8:5-7). The Apostle Paul said that the Spirit and the flesh are at war.

Created in the likeness of the triune God, mankind has a type of trinitarian composition. We have a rational mind, an eternal spirit and the physical capacity to carry out the will of the mind within limitations. The rational mind of man, however, is incapable of fully comprehending the mind of Christ. Within the human mind are located the areas of logic, emotion, and imagination. God gave to Adam both the ability and the order to rule the planet. Adam's mind was far superior to any other earthly creature. As long as Adam used his mind in obedience to God he was able to enjoy paradise and lordship over all other creatures on earth.

Without the indwelling Spirit of God Adam and Eve easily fell prey to their own rational and emotional tendencies. Using her logic, Eve eventually fell prey to the arguments of the talking serpent that persuaded her to eat the forbidden fruit. She also was a victim of her own fleshly desire for the appearance of the beautiful, taste-tempting fruit. She was assured by the serpent that God would not kill her just for eating a piece of fruit. She actually desired to be more like God! Thus her logic, her emotions, and her material desire were useful tools for the cunning of the serpent, which was manipulated by Satan.

Likewise, Adam fell prey to his own logical conclusions. Eve did not die as soon as she ate the forbidden fruit. Therefore, either Adam had misunderstood God, or God had not spoken the truth (Genesis 2:16-17). His emotions could have also influenced his decision to eat the fruit. Possibly he thought that Eve was going to die after eating the fruit, so he ate it to avoid being alone. Whether he exercised simple deductive reasoning or was simply grief-stricken and emotionally over-whelmed, the point is that he acted apart from the Spirit of God and subsequently was disobedient to the command of God. If Adam and Eve had been filled with the Spirit of God, I wonder if they would have given the words of the serpent another thought. Eve would have simply and lovingly instructed the serpent in the error of his reasoning and taught him the Word of God. But she did not possess God's Spirit.

Just as God effectually moves in the universe by the power of His Holy Spirit, mankind affects his earthly domain by the use of scientific ingenuity and physical force. God is Spirit; man is flesh. Being flesh, man is therefore subject to his physiological needs and emotional desires. Man is capable of subjecting his physical yearnings to his intellectual sense of propriety with regard to his societal development. Unlike the beasts of the earth, mankind has the intellectual capability to create governments for the purpose of enjoying a more or less social and civilized existence. However, apart from the Holy Spirit man's rule is ever affected by his emotional dispo-sition and fleshly appetite. Add to this his ability to construct the physical means by which to carry out his will, and it is no surprise that man's legacy is one of war and destruction. Even during the times of the great Crusades men were capable of war and plunder in the name of their god.

God intended that the spiritual component of man serve as a spiritual interface between man and God for man's eternal benefit. When yielded to the Spirit of God, man's spirit would be able to both interact with and be in one accord with God the Father. When logic, emotions, and the physical desires of men operate apart from the influence of the Spirit of God, sin is always the result. However, when the spirit of man is brought to life by the Spirit of God, the various areas of the mind can and will be used by God for the expansion of His kingdom. This process is called regeneration or rebirth. Jesus told a high-ranking Pharisee that, in order to see the kingdom of God, men must be born again by God's Spirit (John 3:3). Jesus was addressing the nature of the spirit of a man. In order for a man to understand spiritual concepts, his spirit must be aware of the things of God. This awareness is brought about when man's spirit is quickened or brought to life by the Spirit of God. Apart from the Spirit of God this rebirth can never occur. Man's spirit is not self-regenerative.

The Holy Spirit was sent by God to usher in the Age of Grace, also called the times of the Gentiles. Jesus told His disciples about the Holy Spirit. He told them that they could depend on the Spirit to lead them into all areas of truth concerning God (John 16:13). The disciples understood that the Holy Spirit, when He came, would empower them to be witnesses of the truth of God's great love for man as demonstrated by the death, burial and resurrection of Jesus (Acts 1:8). Having been witnesses of the Deity of Christ Jesus alone was not enough. They needed the indwelling of God's Holy Spirit for the enormous task of global evangelization. They needed for their own spirits to die and then be resurrected or reborn by the Spirit of God! They would not have to rely only upon their own mortal impressions and perspectives. They would speak the Word of God as His Spirit-filled emissaries to the world!

The filling of the Holy Spirit is exactly the same today. Disciples of Christ receive the same indwelling Spirit for the same task that was begun by Jesus and carried on by many generations of Christians. Genuine disciples of Jesus boldly proclaim the Gospel regardless of the cost to them personally. They never back down when confronted with worldly wisdom, nor do they cave-in or compromise on the precepts of the Word of God, though it may mean severe persecution. They delight in the instruction of righteousness, but never congregate for that purpose without at some time applying the truths they have learned and the joys they have experienced through outward acts of evangelism.

Jesus said that people would receive the power to witness concerning His grace when the Holy Spirit became part of them. People who are filled with the Spirit of God evangelize! They never wear their discipleship as a banner of holiness. They are humbled by the trust the Lord has placed in them. At the same time, they are emboldened by the Spirit of Truth and the urgency of the call of Jesus to spread His Word. They know by the witness of the Spirit in them that Jesus is coming soon. They are never *at ease in Zion!* When Jesus appears,

He will find them faithfully sharing the Word of God that leads to salvation.

It should be noted that mankind has a great capacity for mimicry and imitation. We can mimic nearly every sound we hear. We can imitate the mannerisms of both man and beast. In this way we are able to learn our parents' language and culture. It is this endowment from God that Satan has managed to utilize most effectively in his schemes to destroy mankind and challenge the purposes of God. The Prince of Darkness can easily cloud the imaginations of Biblically illiterate people in accordance with their fleshly appetites. By the exercise of deceit people can be the exact opposite of what they say they are! In other words, people can put on an act! This results in many unregenerate church members honestly believing they are servants of God while they are actually serving the desires of Satan as counterfeit Christians. Though some are actually aware of their lost condition, the majority of church members are simply mimicking their lost parents and grandparents who have always been church members.

Do counterfeit Christians mimic the subtle nuances of genuine believers to the degree that they actually believe themselves to be Christians? Oh yes! However, the charade usually ends during times of bitter dispute within the fellowships of local churches. In fact, the unregenerate church member is always at the bottom of such instances! When confronted with deeper spiritual concepts and challenges that require an understanding of and obedience to the Scriptures, they show not only their snarling fangs, but also their true master's horns! Some of the most highly respected theologians of the

Twenty-first Century have estimated the percentage of counterfeit Christians in American churches at somewhere between seventy-five and ninety percent. That number includes millions of regularly attending church members as well as prominent deacons, beloved pastors, bishops, cardinals, and popes. Some entire denominations miss the mark completely by practicing blasphemy on a daily basis. They blaspheme by denying the deity of Jesus. Others have many of the conventional Biblical graces down to a science, but fail in the more essential doctrines, such as evangelism, discipleship, and the love of God.

After the rapture, many churches will continue their services until Antichrist closes down all organized religious organizations in favor of a one-world religion that worships him. Until then, religious leaders will serve up business-as-usual to their congregations with not even a gnawing intellectual sense that something is different within their communities of faith. Although the true believers will be missing due to the rapture, lost church members will be anxious to believe any and all semi-reasonable explanations for the absence of their few missing friends. Years of denial will serve as the regular rehearsal needed to deny any possibility that they are not true believers. Denial that is never dealt with results in a greater practice of denial.

Surely with the help of the Master of Deception some new Twenty-first Century cult will arise to the forefront following the rapture. It is possible that such a cult even now exists. Their purpose will be to publish a twisted quasi-biblical explanation for the disappearance of so many church members. Without the availability of the convicting power of the Spirit of God it will be easy for many to be completely deceived. It may even be in the form of an edict that God was purging His true church of the fanatical troublemakers. Let's face it. True believers do seem to make unregenerate members uncomfortable! Given Satan's ability to twist the Scriptures to serve his diabolical purposes, reformed cult leadership should be able to use several passages from the Bible to prove their audacious, ridiculous claims. After all, several mainline denominations have been doing it for centuries!

CHAPTER TWENTY-TWO

A CURRENT DECEPTION

In August of 2008 a reformed minister gave a startling lecture to a handful of people at a supposedly Christian retreat. He stated that he had figured out how the people who embrace the idea of a literal rapture of the church were at fault in their theology. For his proof-text he took his audience to the story of Noah and the flood. He asked the people to remember that God sent a flood to carry away all the unrighteous people while Noah and his family were left to repopulate the earth. He then brought their itching ears forward in the Bible to the words of Jesus concerning His discourse in Matthew 24. Jesus said that in the end it would be *as it was in the days of Noah before the flood* (Matthew 24:37-39). The lecturer asked the people, "Now who was taken away, and who remained on the earth?" (DUH!) This man actually taught those unsuspecting people that one day there will be a *kind of rapture*, but that God will take the *unrighteous* out of the earth and will *leave* the righteous behind to build a peaceful world!

If you are thinking carefully right now, you will see how a demonic-spirit-filled non-believer can pervert the Scriptures so that when the rapture does occur and the righteous are taken out, those who remain could actually feel that THEY are the righteous! Diabolical isn't it! Imagine the hardened sinners and vile perpetrators of all manner of indecency that will be left after the rapture! And this man believes that they all will suddenly be transformed into the elect of God! Apparently he also believes that the Antichrist will also be one of the elect of God. At any rate I hope the reader can see how the cover-up is even now being planned by the great deceiver.

The reformed minister in the previous paragraphs has more than a little clout. He begins his retreats by declaring that he is one of Dr. Billy Graham's grandsons. When asked if Dr. Graham is also reformed in his theology, he says that all of the Grahams have always been reformed! Of course, claiming such an influential heritage clearly places him in a position of authority among those who do not know the Bible. Unfortunately for him, it also places a larger millstone around his neck according to the warning of Jesus to all who serve as stumbling blocks. For all false teachers God has reserved the blackness of darkness according to Peter the Apostle (2 Peter 2:17).

Likewise, how might one with such influence be used by the mainstream media to ridicule and persecute evangelistic Christians, thus building a case for their mal-treatment or expulsion? In mid-2006 an infamous comedienne-turned-lesbian-turned-talk-show-host told a national television audience that Christians were as dangerous as radical Islamists!

She was speaking of those *radical* Christians. I suppose that to her a radical Christian is one who neither backs down nor sits in silence when the name of Jesus is scandalized and blasphemed. Of course those who are busy about the business of carrying out the Lord's commission to evangelize the world most certainly should be considered militant!

A person that would even suggest such a notion clearly doesn't understand that radical Islamists seek to heinously murder all non-Moslems (including her!) in order to send them to hell. Radical (true) Christians, on the other hand, seek to lovingly persuade people to die to themselves and thereby live eternally with God. I use the term *true Christian* in the context that Christianity does not recognize varying degrees of followers. Jesus is either Lord *of all,* or He is not Lord *at all!* Christians are only distinguished by displaying their different gift mixes as they press toward the mark of global evangelization.

It must be understood that all practicing homosexuals live in continual disobedience according to the Word of God (Romans 1:22-32). A non-believing, outspoken lesbian blasphemes the name of the Lord Jesus with her rhetoric because she does not possess the Holy Spirit of God as a guide into all areas of truth. If such a person claims to be a Christian and commits such outrageous indignation toward other believers, you can bet there is some colossal denial going on! Therefore, it is not surprising that her words and actions lack any real sense of moral compass. Because of her influential status, she will most assuredly answer to the Living Lord for her role as a major stumbling block. With great power comes great responsibility! From those who have been given much, much is required (Luke 12:48b).

The *Hollywood Affect* is alive and well in America! This affect is achieved when people who have attained stardom through the entertainment media interpose their personal, unqualified, non-spiritual philosophies on their adoring fans. Usually their admirers lap up such drivel and swear by the ridiculous ideologies as if worshipping at the throne of a god or goddess. Hence, the term *matinee idols!* Because Americans are so easily influenced by their Hollywood icons, it should be incumbent upon those who have attained celebrity status to keep their unqualified, incompetent remarks to themselves. In their case an opinion is valuable only in the way that it affects their particular art or performance. As stated before, with celebrity comes responsibility. It is the same with a performer, pastor, or president.

The preceding paragraphs should illustrate how easy it is in America for someone with a growing sphere of influence to openly bash Christianity. Such a person could persuasively point out that militant, evangelical Christians do not represent true Christianity. This might actually be the way it appears to those who have noticed the vast majority of inactive church members. Jesus said that the fields are white unto harvest but the workers are few (Matthew 9:37). When you ask most church members about their personal witness to others, they quickly claim their ignorance as to even how to witness. If you press the issue they proudly announce that their pastor and the missionaries are supposed to do that! Indeed, many are proud to take groceries to a needy family. However, they choke when they find out that the Lord expects them to say they did it was because of their personal relationship with Him! Ministry is only Christian ministry when it is rendered in name of Jesus!

The influence of government is also a huge responsibility. For several decades we have witnessed the growth of an ungodly trend to silence any Christian who insists that the documents of the founding fathers of this nation were profoundly influenced by the Word of God. Even the word *Christmas* has been culturally exchanged for the words *Holiday* or *winter* when referring to the Christmas season. Public schools now observe a *Winter Holiday* break. Major popular retail and discount retail chains now have seasonal *Holiday* sales. They even sell *holiday* trees! Non-Christians now extend *Holiday* greetings! Nativity scenes have disappeared from store fronts due to a government sanctioned ban on overt and offensive Christian representation. Prayer in schools has been reduced to a *moment of silence* so as not to offend non-Christians. The names *Jesus* and *Christ* are becoming conspicuously absent from American society in the Twenty-first Century. Is this a warm-up or dress rehearsal for what it will be like after the rapture?

Because the name of Jesus is the only name under heaven given among men whereby we must be saved (Acts 4:12), it is not surprising to find it banned by the dark powers that are gaining influence over the minds of men. Recently, a Christian recording artist was approached by a major soft drink company. The corporation wanted to use a Christian artist to promote one of its products by attaching a promotional Christian mini-album to a carton of drinks. While the deal was being finalized, the company agent asked if it were possible for the artist to refrain from using any words like *Jesus, salvation, born again,* or any of that *Gospel stuff.* The artist declined the offer because, in his mind, only the name of Jesus makes it a Christian Album. Ironically, the company found a 'Christian' band whose lyrics were void of any vestige of Christianity—including the name of Jesus!

Of course, Christians could possibly relate to such an album by imagining that the text is about Jesus. Unfortunately, proponents of any other New Age religious system could also imagine that the text refers to their particular deity. I say *unfortunately* because the degree of ambiguity on the part of the artist shows that his/her primary concern must be that of making money in a diversified market. That's called prostitution! True Christians faithfully share the Gospel with the name of Jesus as an unmistakable banner. They do not bow to the wishes of those who hate the name of Jesus! To suggest that the name of Jesus be omitted so as not to offend people of other faith systems is to admit that one is ashamed of the Lord Jesus!

An album that could supposedly pass the litmus test for either secular or sacred music is commonly referred to as a *crossover album.* No doubt you have heard the anemic sounds of an artist whimpering, gasping, or moaning out lyrics that could be construed as a persuasive, romantic love song to his or her lover. Ironically, the same song can be marketed today to a Christian audience as the artist's passionate relationship with the Lord Jesus, yet without any direct reference to the name of Jesus!

In a 2006 edition of a Christian music magazine article one "Christian" band member commented that his group found it impossible to use the name of Jesus in their songs without sounding *cheesy!* I'm very sure how his comment registered with the Lord and Creator of the Universe! It may have sounded really cool to others who, likewise, have a problem with the name of Jesus. On the other hand, because it was in a popular magazine, it may have served the purpose of Satan to establish a trend among lesser "Christian" bands! This group is apparently ignorant of the Scriptural proclamation that the name of Jesus is the only means to eternal life (Acts 4:12). They have decided that the name of Jesus is a stumbling block to their purpose. What do you suppose the purpose of a true Christian musician or songwriter should be?

The purpose of all Christians must always be the overt sharing of the name of Jesus with a lost world! The concept of Jesus' name being cheesy is in a different orbit from the Apostle Paul's idea of being all things to all people so that some might be saved. We are to be *Jesus* to all people. His is the only name that gives eternal life. Those who attempt to obscure or omit the name of Jesus are in line with Satan's attempt to keep lost people in darkness by blotting out the light of the world. At the name of *Jesus* every knee shall bow and every tongue shall confess that Jesus Christ is Lord! (Romans 14:11 & Philippians 2:10-11) Jesus! There really is something about that name!

CHAPTER TWENTY-THREE

COUNTERFEIT CARING

Since the bulk of counterfeit Christian denominations are almost exclusively involved in their primary pursuit of social betterment, they will most likely remain deliriously engaged in their own social agendas after the rapture. In the current liberal-political stream of American culture it is possible for a group to plead a deep concern for socio-economic and racial betterment programs and thereby pass oneself off as a *religious institution* or a *church-of-whatever*. While it is true that all Christians must be compassionately and actively involved in ministry to the poor and disenfranchised, the primary mission of the Church of Jesus Christ must first and always be to the poor in Spirit, that is, those who need salvation from their sins. The follow-up ministry to new converts who are also needy is to be considered the church's spiritual obligation under the heading of discipleship rather than that of social compassion. At the risk of seeming hard-hearted I believe many churches direct most of their resources toward meeting peoples' financial and physical needs rather than meeting their spiritual needs. The argument that we must feed their stomachs so they will be able to listen to our Gospel does not take into consideration the fact that "Today is the day of Salvation."

Kingdom-minded believers understand that a few decades of destitution on earth is far better than an eternity of suffering in hell! More than a free loaf of bread, people need the free Bread of Heaven. Feeding people in the name of the church is never the same as feeding people the Word of God in the name of Jesus. If the reader finds this reasoning discompassionate, consider the words of Jesus, who said that there would always be poor people. Jesus said that He came for the poor in Spirit. His mission was not to miraculously feed 5000 men with a small amount of fish and bread (Matthew 14:16-21), but to supernaturally feed the souls of all men with the truth that God loves them and has provided them with salvation from their crippling sins — not their aching stomachs!

Most church members will heartily agree that it is easier to bring a hot meal to a houseful of hungry sinners than to bring empty hands and the Words of life for their starving souls. To do both is ideal; to feed their stomachs but not their souls is sheer disobedience. To assume that providing social programming for a community will result in people lining up at the doors of the church to accept Jesus as Lord is dangerous for both the church and the community. People who believe that accepting Christ means always having a full stomach and a life that doesn't include hardships have received and believed the wrong message! They need only read about the various sufferings of the Disciples and many other Bible heroes.

You may be asking yourself, "How can lost members in a community possibly suffer at the hands of a church feed-the-hungry program? People can easily be deceived by Satan into believing that when they take advantage of the social programs of a local church, they somehow automatically become members of that church by association. The real problem comes when they believe that as members of the church, they automatically become members of the Kingdom of God by association. And why shouldn't they believe this? It is true that many of the churches who provide social programming also throw in a religious service with songs and a devotional message or sermon. It is easy to see how lost people, not knowing the Scriptures, might not fully grasp the Biblical concept of membership in the family of God.

One gross misunderstanding by many poorly educated ministers causes them to preach that Jesus was primarily concerned with taking care of the needs of the poor people of the world. In fact, certain denominational preachers prey on the lower economic types by putting what I call *the blessing-squeeze* on them. They tell them that with a certain amount of *seed* money for an offering; they can receive a huge financial *harvest* from God. This is a primary example of adding injury to insult!

Some ill-trained ministers even attempt to limit their local congregational church memberships to include only people who are not well-to-do socially. Not only do they enjoy being the most educated and *refined* in their church, but they take advantage of the fact that poor people are inclined to risk money on lotto and other get-rich-quick schemes. They know that people with such a mindset will more than likely respond to the pitch about getting a financial blessing if only they will give more sacrificially! When things do not pan out for these members over the long haul, the crafty minister can easily explain that they were not living a holy enough lifestyle for the Lord to bless their investment. If either the manipulative minister or the disenfranchised members had the Holy Spirit within them as a guide, this would never happen!

This author has actually heard an inexperienced pastor proudly announce both in the media and from his pulpit that his church was going to be a *blue-collar church!* That same pastor often privately and publicly remarked at how the poor people he had known throughout his life were truly the salt of the earth. He based his entire philosophy regarding who was worthy to be ministered to on his gross misunderstanding of the Scriptures concerning the poor. He did not understand that James wrote how we are not to show partiality with respect to *any* economic class. That pastor was even reluctant to allow well-educated, financially successful people to have positions of influence on the various church committees. He invested most of his ministerial attention on the lives of a select few who were 'good old boys' that reminded him of those poor saints he knew when he was growing up.

Every true church of Jesus Christ makes Great Commission evangelism its prime directive. This should not preclude ministering to the indigent and unfortunate people in the community around the church. However, the church that has a bigger budget for giving away food than it has for giving away the Bread of Life is not a church of Jesus Christ! The quick social-gospel answer to this statement is that sometimes the people who come to the churches for their Feed-the-Hungry programs and then sit through the required preaching service do at least hear the Gospel! All of this is fine *IF* the church is also going out into the community in an evangelistic effort to reach people for Jesus on a regular basis. The membership in churches that do not have an ongoing, regularly scheduled, evangelistic outreach ministry that also includes evangelistic discipleship training will barely be affected by the rapture of the church.

Perhaps the worst example of church abuse is seen in the latest wave of popular ideas on church growth. Some lost person posing as a minister of the Gospel somehow became very influential. He developed the idea of allowing lost people to attend the services of his church for as long as it took them to 'get saved'. He also decided that it would be better not to preach about the more serious doctrines such as the blood of Jesus, radical change of lifestyle, and personal holiness. This kind of preaching might serve as a turn-off for lost attendees! Imagine the affect of watering down the Gospel message so as not to offend lost people. It is not surprising that such churches grow by leaps and bounds. The real questions should be: What about the power of the Gospel? What about God's warning about light having fellowship with darkness? Isn't the Biblical model for believers all about going out, converting the lost, and then bringing them to the church for the purpose of Christian discipleship?

What should happen if a lost person comes to a Gospel-oriented church of the Lord Jesus Christ? There is no way he or she could sit comfortably and listen to the life-changing truth of God empowered by the Holy Spirit of God designed to convict the hearts of guilty sinners that are desperately in need of a Savior! The paradigm known as the Seeker Friendly approach to church growth is a guarantee that many churches will remain somewhat full after the rapture.

CHAPTER TWENTY-FOUR

RECOGNIZING THE TRUE CHURCH

The average "Christian" church in America in the 21st Century is more like the average social club than what Jesus said His church would be. There are several distinguishing, qualifying characteristics of the true church of Jesus Christ. The primary difference is seen in carrying out the marching orders for the church. Jesus said that His church will have an ever-increasing membership that reaches the ends of the earth (Acts 1:8). His church will have open membership regarding age, race, color, and social position. No member of His church will ever receive preferential treatment by Him or by other members (James 2:1). His church will be distinguished by an inverted hierarchy with regards to its governing. That means the greatest in authority will be the servant of all the other members (Matthew 23:11). Any awards for outstanding service in the Lord's church will only be received after this life. Such rewards will then be cast at the feet of the Lord Jesus in grateful celebration of His glory and worthiness (Revelation 4:10-11). His church will be the only agency that exists solely for the purpose of giving itself away! His church, through faithful witness, will provide the only door (John 10:7) by which people may enter the kingdom of God. His church will never bow to worldly principles and concepts. Instead, the gates of hell will not prevail against its onward march toward global evangelization (Matthew 16:16-18).

Jesus said that His church is the one that, when He reappears, will be found making disciples of all nations, baptizing them in the name of the Father, the Son and the Holy Spirit; teaching them to observe all of His commands (Matthew 28:19-20). Only the true church will be raptured from the earth at the Lord's second appearing. Where the term *Church of Jesus Christ* appears, it should be noted that it addresses individuals as well as the corporate body, which includes all believers in all places.

Members of the true Church of Jesus Christ are recognized as His disciples. The Word of God identifies disciples as those who love Jesus more than they love their blood-relatives, their spouses, or all of the other significant associates in their lives (Matthew 10:37-39). Disciples are identified as those who, by faith, have surrendered their earthly lives to Jesus because of His promise of eternal life with Him in heaven. Disciples are literally those who submit to the Biblical disciplines commanded by Jesus (John 3:36). Disciples are also those who faithfully share the Gospel as proof of their total acceptance of it and reliance upon it. They likewise are actively engaged in the discipling of converts. In other words, disciples take seriously the charge of James to be doers and not just hearers of the Word (James 1:22). They show their faith both in their evangelistic actions and ministry deeds.

They are not doing godly deeds to receive their salvation. They are saved only by the Lord's grace through their faith and therefore, they respond obediently to the commands of the one who saved them with His blood.

Only those who have received the Holy Spirit of God as the directing force for their lives can and will faithfully carry out their ministries as disciples of Jesus. When the Holy Spirit leaves the realm of the earth at the rapture, pseudo-Christians will simply continue faking their relationship with the Holy Spirit. They know about the Spirit in the same way that the demons of hell know about Jesus (James 2:2). They simply refuse to surrender their self-important lives to the will of the Holy Spirit. They are only able to pretend their Christianity on limited bases. These bases include holding important positions in the religious community, restraining their worldly lusts for a limited time on Sundays and Wednesdays, and learning just enough Scripture verses for assimilation into the leadership of a local church. They identify with a local congregation for the purposes of maintaining a respected position in the community and taking advantage of a tax break with their tithes and donations. Their relationship with the local congregation is strictly a one-way street and they own the right-of-way!

While many pretender-Christians come off as soft-voiced, caring, kindly, community-minded types, let's all remember that looks and actions can be deceiving. The Pharisees filled all of the criteria of their day for being perceived as very religious individuals. They appeared so "holy" that the average Israelite greatly revered and often feared them. It is obvious by what they were willing to do to Jesus that they loved the position of authority given to them by the occupying Roman government. Jesus was not fooled by their piety. He called them sons of snakes, white-washed tombs, and lying children of the Devil (Matthew 23:13-30). From His reaction to them we can believe that He is sickened by those today who also do not know Him, but refer to themselves as Christians. Know that every person who attends a church but has no desire to share either the Gospel or their own personal testimony with lost people are hypocrites related to those Pharisees.

The previous description of a hypocrite sums up the religious characteristics of church members that will be left behind following the rapture. One might surmise that these people, upon realization that they have missed the rapture, might be broken in spirit to the point of realizing their need for confession, repentance, and salvation. The problem will be that the One whose purpose it is to move men to confession, the Holy Spirit of God, will have left the earth's realm. People may be truly sorry for their sins of pride and selfishness. However, just like criminals may be sorry they were caught, but not sorry for their deeds, these lost church members will not have access to the Holy Spirit, who gives them the ability to repent and be saved. Will they cry out to Jesus to come back for them? Does Scripture provide for a second rapture of the church designed to pick up those who have seen the error of their ways? Absolutely not! Having seen that the Word of God is true is very different from having not seen and yet having believed the Word of God (John 20:29). That is called faith. Concerning the truth of the Word of God, if you have to see it to believe it, you'll never see it! Neither will you ever be able to believe it!

CHAPTER TWENTY-FIVE

HOW MANY WILL BE RAPTURED?

I have attempted to identify the characteristics and qualifications of those who will be raptured at the end of the Age of
Grace. Sometimes, however, people want more than descriptions. Some need positive identification to determine how
many people will be raptured. Of course, only God knows the
names of the redeemed. They are written in the Lamb's Book
of Life. Because no one can read the hearts and minds of fellow
humans, it is only possible for each individual to know whether
or not he or she will be raptured (1 John 5:13). Although the
Bible identifies the lifestyle indicators of one's relative position before the Lord, only God looks on the heart. Therefore,
whether or not an individual will be part of the rapture, only
God and the individual may know.

There is, however, a general indication as to how many
people will be raptured. It comes from Jesus, the Son of God
and God the Son. While on earth Jesus asked a profound
question. He wondered out loud as to whether He would find

faith on the earth upon His return (Luke 18:18). He was no doubt pondering the difficulty man would have in accepting the challenge of reaching the whole world with the Gospel. Jesus knew things that other men had no way of knowing. However, Jesus said that while He was on the earth He did not know the hour or the day of His return (Matthew 24:36). This may indicate that while on the earth He also could not know the last person who would be saved before His reappearing. He did know that there would be a relatively small number of people that would accept Him as Savior and Lord (Matthew 7:14).

In some of His parables Jesus gave an indication of the proportion of the population that will be saved. In the Parable of the Sower Jesus identified four groups of people and their responses to the Gospel (Matthew 13:18-23). Among these only one group received the truth and was saved. Does that mean only twenty-five percent of the people of the earth will qualify for salvation? Or, does it mean that only twenty-five percent of the people will even appear to be concerned about the things of God?

Jesus also used His Parable of the Ten Virgins to show that people need the Holy Spirit to be included in the Marriage Feast of the Lamb in heaven (Matthew 25:1-13). In this parable ten virgins were awaiting the bridegroom. The virgins were supposed to have lanterns with enough oil to light the festivities of the wedding. Five of them, however, were not adequately prepared for his arrival. When the bridegroom arrived, he took the five who had oil in their lamps into the feast and closed the door. The other five realized they missed the coming of the bridegroom due to poor preparation and frantically attempted to gain entrance after the door had been shut. They were denied entrance and had to face a terrible time of weeping and gnashing of teeth outside of the festivities.

Many theologians have attempted to determine the meaning of the Parable of the Ten Virgins as it may apply to eschatology. Could it be that the ten virgins represent church members who believe themselves to be the bride of Christ and, therefore, worthy of eternal life with Jesus, the Bridegroom? If this is true, is Jesus saying that only half of the people who believe they are Christians will live with Him forever? This percentage is much higher than the numbers expressed by some of the great preachers of this Century. Even so, we now have two figures from Jesus that give insight into how many will be saved. The percentage is approximately fifty percent of twenty-five percent of all the people who have heard the Gospel message. Mathematically speaking, that total is twelve and a half percent.

We also have a major teaching from Jesus that many people will travel the broad road leading to destruction, but only a few will find the narrow gate to eternal life. The equation needed to determine an approximate number or percentage of people that will be left behind after the rapture must include at least one more variable. We must consider that when Jesus mentioned the many and the few in His prophecy, He was considering all of the people from every age since time began. We are now living in a very narrow window of time considering previous ages. If most of those twelve and a half percent have already died, it is indeed a relatively small number that will experience the rapture! In fact, this additional consideration brings the estimates of modern theologians more in line with Jesus' prophecy. It could be that only ten to fifteen percent of the regular to moderately regular church attendees will experience the rapture!

The Southern Baptist Convention currently has a membership of just over sixteen million people. Less than half of these attend services regularly. Fifteen percent of half of fifteen million is 1,125,000 people! This figure is more believable when we read that in 2007 there was only one convert for every 42 Southern Baptists in the State of Georgia! In fact, in 2005 there were less than a million converts reported by the entire Southern Baptist Convention. Many churches in local Baptist Associations have reported no converts during several years! Again it must be stressed that those who are true disciples of Jesus are actively involved in personal outreach evangelism.

Churches that are not actively engaged in seeking the lost for the purpose of converting them by the Gospel of Jesus Christ are simply not His true Church! Christians that are not greatly concerned about the lost condition of most of the people around them have either isolated themselves from the general public or are *cold-hearted religionists.* In either case they are not disciples of Jesus Christ. Churches that believe they must first recruit solid Christian families before they attempt reaching out to the lost in their communities are misguided as to the nature of the church of Jesus Christ. The plain truth is that when a church develops a mind set to reach its community for Jesus, the Lord Himself supplies all of the necessary workers to accomplish the job! Churches that have only an occasional interest in the lost condition of the people in their communities need not be concerned about the rapture of the church. It will come and go and they will continue to ho-hum the urgency of the Gospel of Jesus.

CHAPTER TWENTY-SIX

AMERICA REJECTS THE GOSPEL

The subject of the Rapture of the Church is held in great disdain by many so-called Christian denominations. Most members of mainline denominations are very uncomfortable when the subject arises. Their leaders rarely preach or teach about the Second Appearing of Jesus and the Rapture of the Church. Either the rapture is not addressed in their doctrinal tenets, or the subject is too spooky for the well-tempered ears of their primarily social-gospel oriented members. Even so, the fact that Jesus addressed it often should alert every believer to its relative importance in the overall scope of the Gospel.

Jesus said that no one knows the day or the hour of His coming except for the Father (Matthew 24:36). He also included Himself in His incarnate condition as one who did not know. However, because He said it, we must proceed with the understanding that His coming is imminent. The Apostle John wrote much concerning the coming of Jesus. At the end of John's long life he was able to write in Revelation 22:20, "Amen. Even so, come, Lord Jesus!" Along with John, many

First Century Christians believed that Jesus would come during their lifetimes. They expected His return in the clouds just as the angels had described the event at His ascension (Acts 1:11)! They joyously waited for Jesus to come and save them from their great oppression at the hands of both the Romans and their own Jewish persecutors.

Could it be that mainline Christian denominations avoid any serious discussion about the rapture because it has been wrapped in such mystery? Are they satisfied to consider the Doctrine of the Rapture to be one of the deeper, yet less signifi-cant doctrines of the church? Jesus said that believers should always be ready because we can not know the exact day or hour of His return (Matthew 24:42-44). He also stated that His return would be at a time when we did not expect it. Did He mean that the world would not expect it or that His church would not expect it? Logically it should be understood that those who were not His would certainly never expect it. Those that would never really expect it include all of the followers of false gods, the followers of false christs, and the unregenerate members of both Christian and pseudo-Christian churches.

There can be no separation of the rapture from the Gospel. Therefore, Christians are to live their lives in a way that reveals their constant anticipation of the reappearing of Jesus. We are to watch for the signs of His coming (Matthew 24:33). Jesus commanded His followers to *watch and be ready* for His even-tual and imminent return. There are so many Biblical signs that have been fulfilled that it would take several volumes of very thick books to treat the subject fairly.

Suffice it to say that American society has reached an all-time low concerning morality and an all-time high concerning godlessness. When a so-called Christian nation begins to embrace legislation that enforces both the taking of God out of public schools and the wholesale butcher of the pre-born and partially-born, it can no longer be called a Christian nation. The reason for citing these two government-approved activities is simple. These activities involve slander of the Creator and murder of those that He vows to avenge (Matthew 18:6)!

The description that Jesus gave of life in the last days could be used to describe the very things that are currently taking place in America. The awful truth is that so many godless practices not only meet with government approval, but are enacted into law. If silence in the face of such ungodly legislation is assent, then most churches have given their approval!

If we simply allow our thoughts to drift back to the American cultural scene of the 1950's, we may find ourselves horrified at the rapid downward spiral of morality over the past fifty years. During those former, happier times each public school day began with the *Pledge of Allegiance to the Flag* and either *The Lord's Prayer* or a verse from the Psalms or Proverbs. The Lord's Prayer was also a regular part of every official public gathering, including school athletic events. I can still quote the verses from Psalms and Proverbs that my fourth grade teacher, Mrs. Parr, had us memorize. We learned a lot more than reading, writing, and arithmetic from her and the other teachers! Was it just the customary practice of that time, or did those early childhood mentors know that they were making us better future citizens as well as more thoughtful and respectful elementary school students?

A dissection of the *Pledge of Allegiance* will give us some hints as to its current meaning with reference to the words *one nation under God.* This author advocates *ending* the pledge after the first compound sentence. It should read:

> *I pledge allegiance to the flag of the United States of America and to the republic for which it stands.*

Many atheists have attempted to get legislation passed to have the words *under God* taken out of the pledge. I say that the entire remaining portion should be removed because it is simply no longer true. America is definitely not one nation *under God.* That phrase suggests that God is over the entire nation. It states that there is only one God whose statutes guide and direct the people and, therefore, the government of America. The United States is not a nation under God. Only in the sense that God is over all things could America be considered under God. However, to many citizens the national government is considered to be *above God.* Actually, since the government provides everything for many of the people, it IS their god! To state that we are one nation under God intimates that God is revered and worshipped by the entire nation. Oh that it were so!

The people in America worship many gods; and many people worship no god at all! It is an undeniable fact that people seeking religious freedom settled in America where they could be a nation under God's great and merciful watch care. Likewise, the founding fathers desired to establish a nation where the worship of Jesus Christ could be celebrated under God's protective guidance.

America was begun as a Christian nation guided by the Christian principles found in the Word of God! It cannot be denied that the awesome power of God was openly displayed in both the founding and the protection of early America. God has honored America with great and bountiful blessings in direct proportion to her citizens' collective eagerness to place themselves under His Lordship. Seeing that both our ancestors and our children have benefited greatly from His blessings, it is sad to see how we have chosen to thank our God.

Are we a nation under God? At present there is a movement to strike the name of Jesus Christ, who is our God, from all public forums. Praying and the reading of God's Word for religious purposes have been banned in American public schools. In fact, a High School principal and his athletic director are currently facing criminal trial proceedings. Their crime? At a Booster Club meeting the principal asked the athletic director if he wished to ask grace over the meal. He said that he would, and then he proceeded to offer thanks to God for the food. The American Civil Liberties Union later brought criminal charges and began the process to have the men imprisoned for up to seven years. The two men also face the possibility of loosing their pensions! Why? Because in the public school systems in America all references to God and Jesus must strictly adhere to an historical, non-biblical format, even if no students are present!

In recent times even the word *Christmas* has become taboo in the American marketplace! All government agencies, though initially formed using the Word of God as a moral basis, must now refrain from all Biblical references lest a godless minority be upset by such an affront. If America is a nation under God, which god might that be?

Neither is America a nation that is *indivisible*. Just attempt to discuss any legislative topic with a die-hard Democrat or a staunch Republican and you will see just how politically divided America is! Those Republicans that are morally guided by a philosophy that has been termed the 'religious right,' are usually also strict constitutionalists. They abhor what the Bible calls ungodly behavior. They believe that if a man wants to eat, let him work (2 Thessalonians 3:10)! They are pro-lifers, and they are against homosexual marriages. They desire to govern America in accordance with the statutes and moral convictions of the founding fathers. They desire a small government that does not interfere with the various state governments, unless it is an issue that goes against common decency and the Word of God.

The Democrats sit on the other elected side in the Congress. Though they claim moral integrity, they usually line up on the immoral side of most morality-based arguments. They support homosexual marriage, abortion on demand, and the phantom doctrine called *separation of church and state*. They believe that if a man chooses not to work, he should be entitled to government assistance. This entitlement, many of them believe, should apply to both citizens and illegal aliens.

The Democrat interpretation of the Constitution is much more liberal in that it slants toward socialism. Under the guise of the 'party of the common people,' it promotes a massive central government that supplies all the needs of all the people all the time. It legislatively presses for the redistribution of wealth so that those who have inherited or otherwise obtained wealth are forced by unfair taxation laws to share it with those who have not! All of this is the result of very liberal re-interpretations due to a gross misunderstanding of the views on governing held by the founding fathers.

There also no longer exists *liberty and justice for all* in America. With the recent acceleration toward the appointment of liberal judges, there exists a definite bias toward the philosophies of the Democrats and against the Word of God. Homosexuals and other minorities are backed by organizations that claim to represent the civil liberties of *all* Americans. Shouldn't there always be a problem when civil liberties that promote ungodliness fly in the face of the Word of God and the moral majority in America?

Various civil liberty organizations use their seemingly bottomless slush funds to give legal counsel in cases where the rights of minorities are deemed by them to be in jeopardy. They religiously provide legal counsel for homosexuals, atheists, and other ungodly groups. They engage in a continuous attempt to undermine the intended moral principles upon which both our nation and our government were established.

The largest phony-baloney hoax ever perpetrated upon the citizens of this nation involves a single phrase. The phrase was not included in the early, formal federal papers, but rather in a personal note written by one of the framers of the constitution. The catch-phrase *separation of church and state* was not, does not, nor ever will necessitate the removal of any and all references to God, Jesus, or the Holy Bible from the execution of moral governing ideals. If such a mantra were the established norm for the founding fathers, why was it not mentioned more frequently than once? If, indeed, the mention of God was not welcomed by those who both wrote and defended our constitution, why is the name of the Almighty found everywhere in the birthplace of our freedom and in our nation's capital?

Both the early organization of this country and the Government of the United States of America were founded upon principles set forth in the Bible. Therefore, how could the government operate, and how can the nation survive apart from adherence to and confidence in the godly codes found therein? Who decided there was a better way, and how did they get voted into office with that agenda? The truth is that they were not elected. They were appointed as lifetime justices. Unelected Justices of the Supreme Court somehow are able to change the moral codes, and thus the future course of our nation through ungodly Supreme Court decisions!

From its early beginning to the middle of the Twentieth Century our publicly elected officials were expected to be more than casually involved in one of the several Christian denominations. No candidate for the Congress, the Senate, or the Presidency would have been foolish enough to suggest an agenda that included legislation to remove God and His Word from the public schools. In fact one of the most-used texts in the elementary grades of public school was the Bible.

The moral codes of the Bible were viewed as the backbone of the national moral conscience. The idea of electing to public office anyone who openly embraced a perverted sexual lifestyle was beyond conceptualization. The thought of entertaining the political absurdities propounded by completely unqualified Hollywood personalities was equally foreign to a morally grounded American electorate of a former time. What happened?

How did things get so topsy-turvy concerning right and wrong? When did Americans swallow the lie that says it is wrong for government to seek the wisdom and counsel of God's Word when exercising its authority? Somehow the Federal Court system elected itself to become the conscience of Americans. Instead of a set of godly statutes for our governing, Americans were force-fed ungodly rulings on issues that should have never even been considered issues. With a strong moral code based upon the Word of God in place, most issues are settled before they even become issues. Abominable issues such as homosexual marriage and the murder of the pre-born are condemned candidly by the Word of God.

It was the Supreme Court with its non-elected, lifetime appointed justices that drove the first set of nails in the coffin where America's morals now reside. Their repeated and blatant display of obedience to the ideals of the Prince of Darkness continues to grease the slippery slope that will eventually land most Americans in hell. When one considers the ruling that embraces and protects the wholesale slaughter of pre-born and partially born babies, it is not difficult to see just who is in charge of regulating the moral compass of our nation. Could this happen in a *Christian Nation*? It could not! If this is truly a nation with a government *of, by,* and *for* the people, professing Christians either do not vote, or the majority of voters are not Christian!

It is true that immoral things have taken place since the beginning of the world. The ancient civilizations practiced all forms of abominable behavior. Throughout the centuries humans have practiced abominations from the sacrificing of their own children to fertility gods to the ownership of people for the purpose of sexual bondage and other forms of slavery. Now try to imagine these things taking place among so-called civilized societies. God plainly forbids such!

Even in post-modern times other advanced nations of the world have writhed and danced to Satan's tunes by openly embracing homosexuality and other immoral lifestyles at all social levels. It almost seems that America just can't wait to hear what types of immoral practices are currently in vogue abroad. At present one would find it difficult to distinguish San Francisco from any other of the world's centers for indecency. For such openly flagrant debauchery to be considered normal activity in a nation that God has so richly blessed is undeniably a sign of the end of the Age of Grace. America is ripe for judgment!

Just imagine for a moment how God honored those who at great personal risk sought to establish a nation under His guidelines. Consider the outrageous odds of a rag-tag, all-volunteer, poorly armed Continental Army defeating the greatest army and navy on earth at that time. One eyewitness account told by a British officer is nothing short of astounding! A regiment of the Continental Army was retreating across a dried-up riverbed while a British cavalry unit was in hot pursuit. Suddenly, after the Americans were safely across, the riverbed turned into impassable rapids that blocked the British from following and securing a major victory. What was sure to be a complete rout by the British turned into a miraculous escape by that entire American regiment. The British officer claimed that it must have been the hand of God that favored the Colonials on that day!

The Continental Army consisted of regular soldiers and reservists called Minutemen. The Minutemen were civilians who were ready to fall in for duty at a minute's notice. Nearly every able-bodied male from teenage to senior adulthood was pressed into service to defend the embryonic nation. With God as their sovereign in the place of King George they were driven by a sense of unfaltering patriotism to their country. The defeat of the British and all of the other nations that came against those early American believers in God serves as a testimony to the covenant God is ready to make with any nation whose purpose is to be Christian. Blessed is the nation whose God is the Lord (Psalm 33:12)!

Love for God and respect for His Commandments are major themes found throughout even the earliest documents from which our constitutionalists freely drew. In the writings of the founding fathers one sees the godly ideals that established our principal by-laws and statutes. The framers of our Constitution more than merely hinted at their healthy fear of the Lord. It is safe to say that our country was founded and our nation established by men and women who loved, respected, and worshipped the Lord God of Abraham, Isaac and Jacob. They were believers in Jesus Christ. They daily and purposefully endeavored to live out their beliefs through personal devotion and holiness. Who could possibly argue with God's obvious response to such a people? His sustained blessings upon America are a direct result of His covenant relationship with all who call upon the name of His Son for salvation.

The reader may be pondering or even questioning the possibility of an entire nation united primarily by their allegiance to God. One need only remember the Old Testament stories of how God honored the Israelites as long as they remained true to their part of the covenant relationship with the Almighty. God was faithful even to the point of fighting their battles for them as long as they honored His Commandments. It doesn't take a rocket scientist to figure out the success formula concerning one's relationship with God. When the Israelites were true to God, they enjoyed the abundant living that His blessing brought. When they forsook God's statutes to follow after the pagan gods of the surrounding nations, they experienced drought, military defeat, and eventual exile and enslavement by foreign captors. At this point a modern day prophet should be shouting, "America, beware!" and "America, repent!"

According to Bible prophecy, however, most Americans will not repent. There is only one event that will save American Christians from the wrath that America has been rapidly rushing toward. That event is called the Rapture of the Church. Notice that there will not be a general rapture for all *church members*.

In the rapture only those who have been true in their covenant relationship with God through Jesus Christ will be delivered from the devastating payday known as the Tribulation.

Jesus commissions all of His believers to make disciples of all nations. He commands us to baptize them in the name of the Father, Son, and Holy Spirit. He also commands that those who respond in obedience to His commission must also be actively involved in the process of teaching all newly baptized disciples everything that He has commanded. He then pledges His abiding presence to those who carry out His last general order (Mathew 28:19-20).

CHAPTER TWENTY-SEVEN

STORY III: THE RAPTURE

The reader must have given up by now on the idea that this book will describe what may happen to those who are raptured. Whereas, it is a personal reflection of one's interpretation of the Word, I propose that it is possible to envision the post rapture life of believers (Ephesians 1:17-18). Keep in mind that eyes have not seen, nor ears heard, nor has the mind of man conceived of the things that our heavenly Father has in store for His beloved church in the afterlife (1 Corinthians 2:9-10). However, the Bible states that those things have been revealed to us by His Spirit. That having been said, let us lean on the Words of Truth and imagine the wondrous things concerning the coming event called the Rapture of the Church.

Josh was a friend to all and a member of the First Baptist Church in his hometown. For no apparent reason he had become very interested in recent events in the Middle East. Of particular interest to him was the political climate in and around Jerusalem. He noticed the increased outward displays of hatred toward Israel on the part of militant Islamic Jihadists in the neighboring countries. It had chilled him to the core to hear the Iranian president avow to wipe Israel off of the face of the earth!

A thirty-one year old husband, Josh maintained a disciplined concentration as a dependable and devoted provider for his young family of four. Early in their marriage when he finally got his big chance with a great company, Josh worked faithfully and steadily, never complaining about difficult schedules. The reward for his diligence was that, after only nine years with the firm, he achieved district manager status with his third major promotion.

As Josh had risen through the ranks of the Fortune 500 Company, not once had he compromised his integrity like so many of the other young executives had. He firmly believed that in business, as in every other area of interaction, only honesty and fair treatment would please the Lord Jesus. Josh was a Christian. He had received Jesus as Savior and Lord at the age of eleven, and his life had been dramatically changed forever!

Jesus was so very real in Josh's life that people often remarked as to how they enjoyed hearing him pray at church. The common remark was that he seemed as if he was actually talking to the Lord…like Jesus was really there with him! While others preferred to hear formal, more oratorical public prayers, that was just not Josh's way. He simply loved to talk to Jesus! Because of this perception, many people would often ask Josh to pray for them concerning a problem or illness. Many sought his counsel, not because he was a brilliant young executive, but because he was so very down-to-earth in his dealings with others.

The plain truth of the matter was that Josh really did love people. It wasn't the kind of put-on love that someone learns about at a special *How-To-Love-Others* conference. Josh had approached the books of the Apostle John with a great hunger and passion to find out about God's love. He then applied the Love of God to every area of his life, including his line of business.

Someone approached Josh once with an interesting question. In Sunday School a visitor asked the teacher, "How can a person truthfully say that he sincerely loves everyone?"

As usual all eyes focused on Josh who just smiled and said, "I can't explain why God loves me, but I know He does. Neither can I explain how He expects me to love everyone else, but I know He does. We can love others because God, who loves us, expects us to show our love for Him by our obedience. So we just love others in obedience to His command."

If anyone ever asked Josh about his wife, his joking response was always that he had married well, and much better than she had! Early in life Josh had prayed that God would lead him to the right woman. Likewise, he had prayed to be led by the Lord to the right college, the right job, and every other thing he had ever desired in his life. Since early in his life, his commitment to the Lord to keep himself chaste for his future bride had served to inspire many of his friends to make the same pledge. He had met Judy at their college orientation. As they sat together in that crowded auditorium they both knew that God had answered their prayers concerning their future spouses.

Josh and Judy came from basically the same backgrounds. Their parents were vital members of their respective Baptist congregations. They had honored the Lord by rearing their children according to His commands. Their earthly reward was the joy of seeing their children respond at an early age to the Lord's offer of salvation from sin. Both sets of parents were also gratified to see their children's Christ-like responses to both the difficulties of early childhood development and the peer pressure of their teen years. Both Josh and Judy considered their in-law relationships a sweet gift from the Lord.

Of course, being a committed Christian couple does not mean that life on earth will be a bed of roses. The couple faced their share of heart-breaking situations. Josh had been laid-off from one of his college jobs due to company downsizing. Judy's car had been rear-ended at a dangerous on-ramp resulting in recurring neck problems. Of course, the worst tragedy was the loss of their first child during child-birth. Just after the funeral Judy's first response was to thank God for the chance to carry little Jodie for nine months. Josh was heard many times stating how he couldn't wait to see his first little girl in heaven. The couple spent the next two years speaking at workshops for bereaved young parents and offering private counsel to others who had lost infants.

It was Saturday night. Josh and Judy were relaxing in bed for a moment before reading their evening devotional together. Both of the kids had seemed a little more restless than usual, and getting them to bed had been a chore. They were so excited about Promotion Day in Sunday School. All evening long they had been filled with questions about *who their new teachers would be* and *how far they would have to walk to the sanctuary after class*. Judy was staring out the window at the moon.

"Whew! The kids are finally all tired out," Josh sighed. Noticing his wife's contemplative mood he asked, "Everything okay, honey? You seem a little dazed."

"Oh, it's nothing really," she whispered. "Honey, do you remember last week's sermon; all about the 10 virgins and the coming of the Bridegroom?"

"Um, last week?" He sat up. "You mean the sermon all about the return of the Lord! I think Pastor Mike nailed it! That really was a great sermon. What about it?"

"Well," she responded contemplatively, "do you think Jesus is coming soon. I mean…how soon *do* you think He'll be returning?"

With a surprised look he responded, "Huh? Um… what difference does it make? Sure I think He's coming, and the sooner the better! Why? What do you think?"

She bit her lower lip and eased down into the covers. "Oh, I don't know. It's just…when I think about all of that, I start thinking about the kids, and our folks, and well…how hard it's going to be to give up our life together. It's silly, and I know it, but still…."

Josh turned toward her and smiled. "You know, I bet you're not the only one who is a little anxious about the rapture. I mean…we know all about the joys we've seen in this life. Do we really trust in those promised joys that we can't see?

"Exactly!" She sat up suddenly. "Josh, you really do believe Jesus will come and that we will spend eternity with Him and with each other don't you? Really?"

"Well sweetie," he said confidently, "if I didn't believe that, would we be living our lives the way we do? I mean…would we be sacrificing so much for nothing more than a pipe dream? Now, be careful how you answer. The usual Sunday school response goes something like," he struck a pose with his hands folded as in prayer and his eyes searching the ceiling, "Sure we would, because we're not in it for the rewards. We're just grateful to the Lord for saving us from our sins!"

"Oh Josh," she giggled as she pushed his shoulder, "Come on now! I'm being all contemplative and you're just making fun of me."

"Well," he tried to keep a straight face, "what *do* you think about His coming? Shouldn't it be the greatest thing for all of us?"

"Josh, it *will* be great," she resolved, "I believe it will be just like the Bible says. We will be changed into our new bodies, and we'll meet Jesus in the air along with all of the other believers from all of time!"

"Amen, honey." Josh was yawning, but he absolutely agreed with Judy's proclamation of the truth. Following their brief devotional, a sedated moment of general prayer, and a lingering goodnight kiss the two drifted into a deep sleep. Little did they know that it would be their last night on earth for seven earth years.

At three in the morning Josh awoke for his usual routine. His nightly ramble featured going to the bathroom followed by a trip downstairs for a drink of water and a peek at the thermo-stat. The last leg of his nocturnal duty found him looking in on the kids before making his way back to his bedroom. He had swallowed his usual sips of water and begun his ascent up the stairs on the way to the kids' rooms when it happened.

Many events took place in the span of time that is described in the Bible as the twinkling of an eye. The series of occur-rences began with the unmistakable high-pitched herald of a Baroque trumpet. The sound not only froze Josh in his steps, it seemed to freeze-frame time itself. Josh could not move even his eyes. His instinctive role of family protector was somehow blocked for the moment. Everything melted into a warm bath of light. Simultaneously the stairs, walls, and roof fell away and Josh felt himself racing upward, but without the G-forces normally associated with increasing acceleration.

Josh's eyes were still not operating normally, but both his line of sight and his peripheral vision told him two things: he was not alone and his physical appearance was very different from what it was a moment ago. Emerging from the brilliant light that surrounded him were other beings that he instantly perceived as humans. At first he was amazed by the brilliance of their form. More amazing was the fact that, even though the people that now surrounded him were very different from any people he had ever known, he recognized every one of them.

At first Josh's mind reacted to the familiarities of his deceased relatives like one who is warmed by a fond memory. Almost immediately, however, he understood that these familiar forms were not just resemblances of his dead grandparents.

The two forms in question were definitely his grandparents and they were definitely alive! They were alive, and they were there with him! They were all there together…somehow, somewhere, but not on the earth!

Suddenly Josh realized that he was able to not only move his eyes and his head, but that he was also able to turn his new body. Although he had nothing solid on which to stand, he could, by thinking it so, move in any direction at any speed. His next thoughts were of his Judy and their children. Immediately they were all with him; even little Jody! He had not missed them. He had simply not had time to think of them. Everything to this point had happened within a split second. But when he thought of them, there they were! He began to think of other people, and sure enough, everyone he thought of was instantly with him. The amazing thing was that his thoughts were only of the good and great people in his life.

Josh was not conscious of the fact that he neither had thoughts of anything bad nor of anyone who was not with him. Amazingly, his thoughts were only of good and great things. The absence of stress, dread, pain, and sorrow caused him at last to realize what must have happened. He had been raptured out of the world of sin and into the promised realm of peace!

Josh knew the Scriptures well enough to know that everything the Apostle Paul wrote concerning the rapture had taken place. His next thought was one of joyous anticipation. Paul had written that the dead would be raised first and then those who were alive would be changed and caught up in the clouds with them. And they would be forever with Jesus! At that moment he was looking into a face more wonderful than any face he had ever encountered. Though he had never seen the face before, Josh knew exactly who it was that now smiled at him. The smile of the Savior erased every confused or angry thought Josh had ever had.

Josh at once understood the love that God had for him and the price God had paid for his salvation. He was totally immersed in a sea of peace. Rather than weep as a result of a flood of physiological and psychological human emotions, Josh summed up his eternal love and gratitude with the words of Thomas, the disciple. Without physically saying a word, Josh's soul exploded from deep within him with the ultimate words of submission and commitment, "My Lord and my God!"

Josh understood immediately that the essence of his new body was not just connected to the Lord; his life force was actually flowing from the Lord. Apart from the Lord he would have no reason to exist. On earth he had sought to please the Lord with acts of obedience, but that service was marred by distractions, interruptions, and his own limitations. In this realm he was able and delighted to devote every fiber of his being to pleasing the one who supplied him with the excellent existence he now experienced.

There were no arguments or questions to clutter his perfect existence. His life was simply a matter of obedience to his God. His obedient attitude was not hampered by thoughts of inadequacy or potential failure. He was completely confident that whatever the Lord required of him would be within his ability to accomplish effortlessly.

Josh had no anxious sense of wondering what the Lord would require of him. In fact, the Lord was always lovingly speaking to him, lovingly instructing him, lovingly assigning him tasks, lovingly encouraging him and lovingly praising him. There was no sense of passage of time because time had ceased to be relevant. There were no regular cyclic periods with times of waking and sleeping. Because there was never any darkness, there was no sense of day or night. In fact, there was no sense of time at all! There were no rest periods due to the fact that his new body required no rest. Work that may have been considered tedious, boring, or monotonous on earth was considered a delightful opportunity to obediently serve the Lord.

Josh looked forward in grateful anticipation to each of the Lord's assignments because each mission was always crystal clear. Every task was carefully designed by the Lord according to the demonstrated faithfulness of each person. The assignments were in the form of rewards based on the level of faithfulness to the Lord's commands while ministering in His name while on earth. Therefore, each believer was rewarded proportionately for his or her level of commitment to the Lord's commands. The rewards manifested themselves in the types and degrees of tasks given by the Lord. Each laborer was always extremely aware of the strategy of the Great Commander of the hosts of heaven. Each task involved preparation for the Lord's Second Coming.

Many of the responsibilities involved a briefing of the more faithful and fruitful among the church as to their roles in the governing of the Lord's new Kingdom on the new earth. It was a great joy for all of the raptured church to see Bob, someone who had been a shy shoe salesman on earth, being trained to rule over a large province within the new Kingdom. While on earth the smallish, sickly man had not been able to participate in organized sports programs nor to serve in the military. He had, however, been faithful in all things concerning his commitment to Jesus, his Lord. He had led scores of children to faith in Jesus during the many years he served as a Junior Department Sunday School teacher. Bob had also been an active witness by sharing the love of God with everyone he ever knew. Many of the children he had led to Christ and discipled were also training now alongside him for their respective regions of responsibility in the new Kingdom.

For the first time in Josh's existence there was a complete absence of stress. There was absolutely no pressure concerning anyone's expectations of him. Likewise, on his part there was no concern regarding production deadlines, other workers, or scheduling worries. He knew that his work was acceptable. He knew that he was the only one that could do his job like he could do it! He had the joy of using his unique level of giftedness to accomplish perfectly what the Lord had awarded him the chance to accomplish for His Kingdom. One thing that he truly would have enjoyed knowing was that all of the world's concerns and problems were gone from his life forever. I say 'would have enjoyed knowing' because all such thoughts about the problems of his former life on earth were forever dissolved in the moment of his rapture.

Josh was definitely not a mindless worker bee in some cosmic hive. He still had initiative, enthusiasm, and desire to excel at whatever he attempted. The difference was the fact that he absolutely loved doing whatever he could do to please the Lord who had saved his soul! Concerning his former human ideals, he still enjoyed the sweet fellowship with other members of the raptured church. He still appreciated his special relationship with Judy, his children, all of his relatives, and other close associates from the earth. The primary difference was that after seeing the one who died to provide him and his family with eternal life, his eternal objective was that of complete obedience to the Lord's commands. The greatest joy that Josh and Judy would ever know was the joy of serving the Lord together with their children. All hearts were keenly fixed on pleasing Jesus, their Savior and Lord! The ecstasy they found in that relationship was far superior to any earthly desire they had ever dreamed of. Each was completely fulfilled in their new heavenly relationship.

Everyone's joy was fixed firmly on completing the preliminary tasks that the Lord had assigned. The assignment process was nothing like the verbal process used on earth. Each individual was motivated by a supreme sense of warmth and well-being that came from knowing exactly what to do and how to do it. It was as if the Lord was constantly directing and affirming each of His eternal family members. Because of each individual's earthly preparation, the sensation was that of having done the tasks before. The difference was that this time the Lord Jesus was personally involved with their individual projects. The term *work* did not apply in the sense that it was used on earth to describe labor. The earth-term *rest* was a better description of the work done by the redeemed. Neither were the terms hungry, weary, sleepy, angry, or frustrated included in the vocabulary of the raptured church.

It was very clear to all that the earth was going through a period of great tribulation. They were not discompassionate concerning those on earth who were suffering through the awful period. However, their goals and assignments were their primary focus. Everyone knew that they would be accompanying the Lord on His return to earth at the end of the time of tribulation. They each knew how they would participate in His new Kingdom on earth. They also knew that they would be completely prepared for their part in the thousand-year reign of Lord Jesus on earth. Each person knew what every other person would be doing. There was neither envy nor the idea that someone might be better suited to do the work assigned to another person. All relationships were celebrated at the highest degree of excellence. There was only the joyous community of the raptured church, and all things were done for the glory of their God, Jesus Christ!

CHAPTER TWENTY-EIGHT

THE JUDGMENT

The previous chapter has dealt with the author's ideas pertaining to the condition of believers during and immediately following the rapture. Some sense of what the church will be doing following the rapture has also been suggested. The Apostle Paul wrote that men have an appointment with death, after which comes the Judgment. Whether he meant that Judgment would occur immediately following death or that Judgment was impending and would occur at some point after death is not certain.

A pragmatic interpretation of Paul's writing would insist that the very next thing following the moment of one's death would be his or her judgment. However, another possible interpretation maintains that death is the great dividing line, after which there are no more chances to change one's final position before the Lord. After a person dies, therefore, his or her judgment is set. If we accept the suggestion that time ends and eternity begins for those who die, then the matter of *when* the Judgment occurs is not arguable since the concept of time will have changed. Attention must then shift to the order of after-life events. Apart from the passing of time, even the order of events has little significance. The order is only significant depending on whether one is a believer or not!

Paul also wrote that he was confident to be absent from the body, and to be present with the Lord (2 Corinthians 5:8-10). This passage verifies that time does end and that for believers the time of Judgment may occur simultaneously. The sense of being present with the Lord suggests an eternal presence. This truth is inferred by the fact that Paul is addressing believers in his letter.

Perhaps Paul's greatest contribution to the peace of mind of believers is in his crystal clear summary of the rapture found in a letter to the Thessalonian church (1 Thessalonians 4:15-17). He wrote that there will be a call from the archangel resembling a trumpeting. The Lord will then summon all who have placed their faith in Him, both the dead in Christ and those who are still alive, to come to Him in the air. Christians whose earthly lives have ended previously will ascend from their graves first. The bodies of those who are still functioning will be instantly changed to accommodate their ascent into the realm of heaven. All of the raptured church will then meet with Jesus in the realm of heaven. The idea that a type of judgment has already occurred is seen in the fact that those who meet with Jesus in the air will be with Him forever.

Jesus spoke of several courtroom-like scenarios. In one scene He related the difference between pretender-Christians and true Christians (Matthew 25:31-46). He used sheep and goats in His depiction. The goats and sheep were separated in this post-rapture judgment scene. Jesus offered a mysterious, metaphorical analogy by describing Himself as being hungry, thirsty, a stranger, naked, sick, and in prison. His judgment of the sheep was that they displayed mercy toward Him when they cared for Him in these helpless conditions. The sheep are surprised when He reveals that caring for the least of His brethren is the same as caring for Him.

His judgment on the goats was that they did not display mercy toward Him while He suffered in these helpless conditions. The goats respond only with self-righteous questioning of the Lord's judgment. Their indignant defense is that they never saw Jesus in any of these dire situations. Jesus lets them know that they failed the test of compassion by not caring for His brethren that they have actually seen in these conditions.

The goats are cast into outer darkness where there is weeping and gnashing of teeth. The sheep are welcomed into their eternal life with Jesus. The goats could represent those who pretend to be Christians. They separate things done *for* the church house and *at* the church house (supposedly for Jesus) from kindness and acts of compassion toward those who may not be associated with the church house. Jesus loved sinners and died to demonstrate His love for all. Goats self-righteously distance themselves from the sinners who are less fortunate than themselves, but that Jesus died for!

Sheep, on the other hand, are great imitators of their Good Shepherd. Jesus gave His life for them; therefore, they give their lives for others. Sheep do not see themselves as deserving of God's love. Sheep love much because they have been forgiven much (Luke 7:47)! Sheep do not have to understand the theology of Christianity; they only need to follow the example set by their Shepherd. Sheep do not have a qualification checklist to determine who deserves their kindness and mercy. Sheep simply do as they were commanded by their Shepherd. They love!

Although the 'sheep to goats' comparison that Jesus was making referred more to the world's treatment of His actual brethren, Israel, I believe it can also apply to a 'believers to non-believers' comparison. Believers are referred to by Jesus as His sheep who hear His voice. He also uses sheep in other metaphorical parables of the kingdom. My favorite example of believers as sheep comes from the Twenty-third Psalm. Jesus is the Great Shepherd for all believers!

Another form of judgment pointed out by Jesus was described in several of His parables about talents and possessions. His simple judgment was that much is required of him who has been given much (Luke 12:48). In the parables, those who increased the kingdom of the one who entrusted part of it to them were judged worthy of eternal joy for being good and faithful servants (Matthew 25:20-28). The judgment on those who failed to yield growth with what was loaned to them was quite different. That which they had was taken from them and given to those who had increased the kingdom.

Likewise, those to whom a King had shown mercy by forgiving their indebtedness to Him were judged as merciless if they would not also forgive their own debtors (Mathew 18:23-34). The King rightfully treated them the same way they had treated those who were indebted to them. They were cast into a place of punishment with no way to ever repay their debt.

Perhaps the most memorable of the Lord's parables concerning judgment is the one about the rich man and the beggar (Luke 16:19-31). Although the rich man had all of this life's pleasures according to his great wealth, he was judged guilty by the Lord for not caring for poor people such as Lazarus, the beggar. No doubt he knew about the impoverished condition of the destitute Lazarus. Lazarus was not only hungry, but had great sores, possibly leprosy. The rich man was indeed acquainted with his fellow human's condition, but chose to exercise neither compassion, nor mercy, nor generosity. His judgment included an eternal verdict of separation from both God and Lazarus in a place of fiery torment. Because Jesus mentions no other crime the rich man had committed, we must believe his crime was apathy toward suffering mankind. It should be a relief to some to know that men will not be judged for having great wealth, but rather, for what they do with it!

Many believers have been swept away recently concerning a very slippery doctrine. Believers are assured by the words of Paul under the influencing leadership of the Holy Spirit that they will not face eternal condemnation. However, there is much discussion about another judgment that they will face. Many Christians spend anxious moments worried that Jesus will show all of their evil actions while everyone looks on! They obviously have forgotten that Jesus proclaims their innocence when He faithfully forgives their sins upon their confession and repentance. He separates their sins from them as far as the east is from the west (Psalm 103:12). He promises to remember them no more (Isaiah 43:25)! Therefore, how can God judge a sin that He no longer remembers?

Let's be sure of one thing. If All-knowing God forgets something, it can only be because *He has chosen* to forget it! When God looks upon a confessing, repentant sinner, He sees only the blood of Jesus that washes away the sin and cleanses that sinner of all unrighteousness! He sees only the righteousness of Jesus! That is how we are made the righteousness of Christ! The judgment feared by ignorant believers, therefore, is in actuality only His basis for their future kingdom assignments. At that appointment, God, in accordance with His perfect knowledge, will award various positions of responsibility to raptured believers. The awards will mirror the kingdom work attempted by those faithful believers during their lifetimes on earth.

Our willingness to do God's will is always in exact proportion to both our trust in Him and our commitment to His Word. Believers should display no fear regarding the judgments of God. Believers simply attempt the work of the kingdom in accordance with their level of faith in their King. We must all continually ask the King to increase our faith. Be confident, however, that when you ask for increased faith in God, the trials that bring about that increase in your faith will surely come! And they will come through God with His permission!

The Lord Jesus delivered the ultimate decree as to His judgment concerning the true church. The Apostle Paul, under the influence of the Holy Spirit, said that there is no condemnation for those who have placed their faith in Christ Jesus (Romans 8:1). Concerning judgment Paul said that believers will be used in the exercise of various forms of judgment. Some believers will be used in the process of judging nations and angels (1 Corinthians 6:2-3). This statement was made pertaining to the church judging matters of disobedience within the local congregation. However, It is also associated with Paul's proclamation that believers will reign with Jesus (2 Timothy 2:12). That believers shall reign with Jesus was also sung about by the twenty-four elders according to John's vision (Revelation 5:9:10). John believed that Jesus had made believers to be kings and priests unto God (Revelation 1:6). This must describe the role of believers during the thousand-year reign of Jesus after His return following the Tribulation.

I believe that during the seven years of tribulation on earth following the rapture, the glorified church will be engaged in an intensive program of preparation. Because time will have a different meaning in the realm of heaven, it is impossible to understand its parameters. However, because God has always prepared a people for His purposes, it is reasonable to assume that following the rapture believers will receive their assignments and their training for areas of responsibility within the new kingdom.

The capital of the new kingdom will be Jerusalem, which will serve as the Lord's center of government. He will rule over the earth for a thousand years while Satan is chained in a pit. Those who have been raptured, including Enoch and Elijah, will assist in the glorious reign of the Lord over all the earth.

CHAPTER TWENTY-NINE

THE DEAD IN CHRIST

Clarification must be made concerning the proclamation of the Apostle Paul that at the rapture the dead in Christ shall rise first. The word *dead* ceases to exist in the vocabulary of those who have placed their faith in the Lord of Life! According to the words of Jesus there is no death for Christians. He defeated Death and the Grave with His resurrection! The moment a Christian accepts Jesus as both Savior and Lord is the very moment that eternal life in Jesus begins.

It is easy to understand the great degree of concern expressed by First Century believers at the passing of their loved ones. Jesus had promised eternal life for all who accept Him as the Son of God and God the Son. His words, spoken to Martha at the tomb of Lazarus, were, "He that believes in me, though he were dead, shall live. And he that lives and believes in me shall never die" (John 11:25-26). Jesus gave the perfect object lesson to prove the first part of His quotation moments later by resurrecting Lazarus, who had been dead for four days. Even more dramatic proof was given by His resurrection! Imagine the glorious scenes provided for those who saw Him ascend to heaven and then heard the angelic proclamation that He would return in the same manner in which He departed (Acts 1:11).

Then days turned into weeks, months, and years and people who had believed in Jesus began to pass away! According to Apostolic teachings, these believers weren't going to die. But they died and were buried! First one, and then others followed in what must have seemed a contradiction to the teachings of Jesus. Paul, always concerned about the spiritual health of the early church, responded to the growing anxiety of many by writing his Spirit-filled explanation (1 Thessalonians 4:16-17).

According to Paul, the Lord definitely would return for His church. At His return, the dead would rise first, followed by those who were still alive, whose bodies would be instantly changed so as to accommodate the infinite differences between earth and the eternal realm. The only possible way to harmonize Paul's prophecy and the words of the Lord Jesus is to believe that those who die in Christ *do not die* according to the traditional world view. Yes, they cease to function as mortal beings. Yes, their physical vital signs are absent. No, they cannot respond to external stimuli. According to every County Coroner they are clinically dead. But are they spiritually dead? No. Jesus, who is God, cannot lie!

The explanation requires some out-of-the-box thinking; so, here goes! The most difficult concept to shake off for mortals is the incompatible concepts of time versus eternity. Our lives are made up of a parade of events passing chronologically on a time line. Another way of stating it is *earthly life takes time.* As mortals, our lives are more or less ruled by the amount of time that we have during our work day to get things done. Because time presents us with certain parameters, we find ourselves at the mercy of good scheduling habits. Due to a variety of time constraints, stress build-up is a major cause of many physical and emotional problems in modern industrialized societies. In view of these time-related factors it is difficult to even imagine an existence that is not governed by time constraints. Can you imagine a timeless realm called eternity?

We must think of it in terms of *realms*. Because chronological time ceases for those who pass out of the earth realm and into the eternal realm, the believer is never aware of his or her passing. The seamless transition provides no awareness of life ending on earth and continuing in heaven. There can be no sense of dying because death does not exist for those who believe that Jesus has given them eternal life. Christians have already experienced the death of their sinful selves on a daily basis since the time they accepted Jesus as Savior and Lord. They have already died to their sins. Hence, there can be no more death.

For believers death is merely a haunting shadow without substance. Someone may argue that since the Bible tells of Jesus' victory over death, there is no more death for anyone! It must be stressed that death is the result of sin. Therefore, where there is sin, there is death (Romans 6:23)! In the spiritual realm death is described as separation from God. Jesus' death and resurrection have provided mankind with the possibility of a restored relationship with God. Where sin has been forgiven and eradicated by the blood of Jesus, there can be no death. In that sense, death has been defeated or cancelled by the capable work of Jesus. He died so that we may live with Him eternally. All who accept Jesus' death as their own death to sin and His resurrection as their own resurrection to eternal life are born again in Him and will never die!

The psalmist wrote, "Yea, though I walk through the valley of the shadow of death, I will fear no evil, for You are with me" (Psalm 23:4). From the moment of our spiritual rebirth, the Lord never leaves us because His Spirit lives in us. At the moment of our rebirth we are recreated fully and forever alive by His Spirit!

From the believer's perspective, therefore, the next thing that will happen is the sound of the trumpet of the archangel (remember Paul's prophecy in 1 Thessalonians 4). Even though years, decades, even millennia have passed for those in the mortal realm, no time will have passed for those in the immortal realm. In other words, if a believer loses his/her mortal life, at that precise instant their eternal life resumes with Jesus at the rapture. Their life remains uninterrupted by what unregenerate mankind refers to as death. Remember the words of Paul in another address of the subject. He said that he was willing "to be absent from the body, and to be present with the Lord" (2 Corinthians 5:8).

The Author of Hebrews wrote that it is appointed unto man once to die, but after this, the judgment (Hebrews 9:27). Obviously Paul believed that life for believers was a glorious, eternal process which cannot be interrupted even by death. He understood the seamless passing of a believer from our mortal realm into God's eternal realm. He also believed our judgment to be constant, and that God has always known the final outcome for everyone.

God can't help but know all things; He's Omniscient God! The idea of man dying once can only refer to man's eventual departure from the physical world. When people cease to function biologically, from a purely physiological perspective, they are assumed to have died. The physical bodies of believers will either die or be changed at the rapture because they must be fitted for eternal existence.

How does the concept of life without end work when applied to non-Christians? Upon their departure from the earth realm, those who have rejected Jesus as Savior and Lord will face the Great Day of Judgment (Romans 2:16). Because God is holy and just, those who refuse to accept His offer of restoration through Jesus Christ will die an eternal, spiritual death, which is separation from God. Upon their demise in the earth realm, they will be consigned to the eternal realm of hell with their sins intact. Having never accepted the blood of Jesus as a covering for their sins, they will have rejected God's offer of eternal life with Him in heaven! If they never admitted that Jesus is their only Savior and their Lord, they remain separated from God for eternity! If they never forsook their daily, sinful lifestyles in favor of a life of holy submission to the Lord Jesus, they will experience a spiritual death which is eternal separation from God! They will be alive, but they will have opted for an eternal life of fiery torture and agonizing regret in a place from which there is neither relief nor escape. It is the fiery place of the second death (Revelation 20:14-15)! They will have died physically on earth and then they will commence the processes of dying spiritually (separated from God) and suffering physically in hell for eternity.

Because Heaven is the perfectly holy dwelling place of the perfect and holy Lord God Almighty, it is a realm where neither sin nor sinners may exist! Because God is righteous, He rejects sin. Because He is the true and righteous judge, He must pronounce judgment on all sin. At the Judgment, God will personally reveal to each sinner every one of his or her sins. These sins represent unarguable reasons why the sinner cannot enter Heaven. They also reveal that the sinner has condemned *himself or herself* to an eternity in a place created for the punishment of Satan and his followers (Matthew 25:41). If you are not following Jesus, you are following Satan!

Satan's followers are those who choose not to follow the Lord. Some of the angels chose to align themselves with Satan against God. For their disloyalty they were ejected from God's presence in heaven (Revelation 12:9). Likewise, human beings unwittingly align themselves with Satan as long as they reject God's gracious offer of eternal life. You may ask, "Why can't a person just remain neutral?" The reason is clear.

Though it may have escaped the notice of many, this world was created by God for His glory (Psalms 29:2)! Therefore, all people are given the choice to either accept or reject God. No one is exempt from the process of choosing. God offers everyone the chance to restore their eternal relationship with Him through the forgiveness of their sins made possible by the atoning death of His Son, Jesus Christ. Rejection of God's offer of forgiveness is acceptance of the eternal consequence of damnation.

Therefore, at the passing of a nonbeliever, instant judgment follows resulting in judicious consignment to hell. Unrepentant sinners will spend eternity in hell for at least two reasons. The atheist chooses to ignore God's glory as displayed in the creation (Psalms 19:1) thereby choosing to believe that there is no God. Others, including many church members, have acknowledged, as have all the demons, the fact that God in Christ exists, but unwisely choose to reject Him as Savior of their eternal souls and Lord of their mortal existence. While some church members welcome Him as their Savior, they refuse to make Him their Lord. Because of His death for the sins of mankind Jesus already is the Savior of the world. Faith in Him exists only when you make Him Lord of your life.

God does not desire that anyone made in His image perish in the flames of eternal punishment (2 Peter 3:9). It must be stressed that the realm of hell was not created for mankind. According to the Scriptures hell was created for Satan and his fallen angels. However, since there are no eternal realms other than heaven and hell, those who choose to reject Jesus as Savior and Lord doom themselves to eternal punishment in a devil's hell.

The process that follows can be deduced from several Scripture verses. The Bible affirms that it is appointed unto man once to die after which comes the Judgment (Hebrews 9:27). Logically then, if you do not die, there is no Judgment for you. Jesus said that those who believe in Him will never die (John 11:26). This statement abolishes death for believers. In fact, Paul wrote that there is now no condemnation for those who are in Christ (Romans 8:1)! Concerning believers Paul also wrote that he was willing to be absent from the body, and present with the Lord (2 Corinthians 5:8).

In other words, according to the Spirit-inspired writings of Paul, when a mortal being's body expires, time ceases to be relevant. Time as we now understand it ends, and eternity begins. We know this because of the Genesis account of the creation of man. God breathed into Adam's nostrils and he became a living soul (Genesis 2:7). Not only his soul, but the souls of his entire race are eternal in their nature, having been created in the likeness of Eternal God. Following an appointed number of days on the earth, the souls of men will continue to exist either in heaven or hell... two timeless, eternal realms.

If the above mentioned concepts are true, the following becomes an accurate account of the eternal process of a non-believer. At the point of physical expiration individuals who have rejected God's offer of eternal life in Jesus will find themselves facing the Lord for their eternal Judgment (2 Corinthians 5:10). Judgment will be based on the individual's deeds which represent his or her choices. The Book of Revelation describes the scene. In John's account of the Judgment, several books will be opened. Contained in some of the books are all of the deeds and words of every non-believer (Revelation 20:12-13). Since God is a timeless being, and their sins have never been covered by the blood of the Lamb of God, all sins against Him will exist as if they were in the process of being committed! The universal law of God states that the wages of sin is death (Romans 6:23). The massive amount of sinful evidence against each non-believer should leave no room for disagreement.

After the review of the individual's sins, another book, the Lamb's Book of Life, will then be opened. Contained in this book are the names of all who have placed themselves under the applied blood of the Lamb of God and received His forgiveness for their sins. Everyone who is raptured will find their names in this book! All who have confessed Jesus as Lord and believe that God has raised Him from the dead will find their names in this book! However, all whose names are not found in the Lamb's Book of Life will be cast from God's presence into eternal punishment (Revelation 20:15). Is your name in the Lamb's Book of Life? If not, it can be!

Imagine the eternal sorrow and disappointment of those who lived their lives as if they would never have to answer for their sins. Imagine the horror in the hearts of those who thought of God as either a *doting grandfather* in the sky or as *the man upstairs* rather than the Righteous Judge to whom they shall be required to give an eventual accounting. Imagine the surprised church members who played church well enough to win an Academy Award but never surrendered their lives totally to the King of Kings and Lord of Lords!

Most people will not even know that the rapture has taken place. This statement gains credibility in the light of one of Jesus' most quoted parables. In the Lord's parable about the beggar Lazarus, a rich man dies and his torment in hell is described. We may suppose that when someone is consigned to hell, he or she would be a little wiser after the truth sounds forth the indictment. And yet, this condemned man is still expecting others to do as he so bids. He orders Abraham to send Lazarus (whose infirmities he indignantly ignored on earth) with a drop of cool water for his parched tongue (Luke 16:24). He still must not realize what has happened! He only knows that he is suffering, and that he doesn't want his brothers to suffer in such a place! In truth he is simply acting like those who have never received the Spirit of God.

Without the Spirit, people only recognize they have done something wrong because of their punishment. Any guilt associated with their punishment is due to their breaking of parental rules or other kinds of societal codes. Their hearts are not affected by the wrongs they inflict on others because their wills remain unbroken. Therefore, given another chance at freedom, they will most likely continue their unrighteous acts against both God and humanity. Apart from the Spirit of God there is only a spirit of lawlessness (sin) which constantly wars against the Spirit of God (1 John 3:4)! The spirit of lawlessness comes from Satan who continues to rebel against God. He influenced other angels to sin against God. Likewise, he tempts and influences mankind to sin against God.

There are many belief systems that embrace the teaching that it is solely man who rebels against God's laws. Those who teach this are either oblivious to the fact that God created man in His own image, or they do not believe man is influenced by Satan and his fallen angels. It is Satan who has blinded the latter group. If he can persuade man that there is no devil, and also that man is totally depraved apart from any satanic influence, he can enjoy a free hand in his reign of terror in the affairs of men on earth.

As to the deeds of men, Jesus told several instructive parables describing the foolishness of people who live their lives as if a Day of Judgment was not rapidly approaching. In some parables, servants did nothing with the gifts or talents entrusted to them by their master. In other parables, men used their resources solely for their own enterprises while completely disregarding the dire needs of other people. Some people did not love anyone but themselves and their relatives. Jesus also said that anyone who did not love Him above all others on earth (including relatives) did not qualify as a disciple (Luke 14:26). Jesus said that a man can only gain eternal life in heaven if he is willing to lose his own life in this world for the sake of the Gospel (Luke 17:33). Without the sacrifice of one's life for Jesus, every other religious act is nothing but a charade.

Aside from the people mentioned in the parables there are the noticeable types who engage in the sinful lifestyles that will exclude them from eternal life with Jesus. In the letters of the Apostles Paul and John are included several lists containing degenerative, immoral activities by which people can disqualify themselves from participation in the eternal Kingdom of God (1 Corinthians 6:9-10; Galatians 5:19-21; 1 Timothy 1:9-10; Revelation 21:8). In the book of Revelation, the Apostle John also lists the types of people who will be excluded from everlasting life in heaven (Revelation 22:15). Both John and Jesus drew much attention to the satanic act of lying (John 8:44). The simple truth is that anyone who practices sin as a lifestyle by refusing to yield daily to the Lordship of Jesus can not inherit eternal life! As bad as the act of sinning may be, it is not the entire problem. We all sin! It is the refusal to acknowledge our sins, confess them to God, and then turn away from those sins that distinguishes lost people from believers. When we sin, we must confess our sins to Jesus in remorseful repentance. Jesus has promised to forgive our sins and cleanse us from all unrighteousness (1 John 1:9).

In the language of Biblical Judgment non-believers are referred to as *the unrighteous*. Since they have not submitted themselves to the lordship of Jesus, God does not view them through the righteousness of Christ. They are viewed by God as unrighteous. The rapture will have no effect on the unrighteous. They will continue, and most likely increase, all of the sinful activities in their lives. Incidents of murder and other forms of immoral violence will greatly increase following the Rapture of the Church. This will be due to the increase of lawlessness, the absence of godly moral conscience, and the absence of the protective presence of the Holy Spirit.

During the closing years of the Great Tribulation constant catastrophe and war will account for millions of deaths. At the point of death these souls will be instantly judged guilty for not embracing the gift of eternal life that was repeatedly offered to them when the Church and the Spirit of God were present on the earth. The Great Tribulation is the first part of their judgment. From the perspective of countless unrighteous people who have died throughout the ages, they are receiving their eternal punishment while you are reading this book. They did not go to a mythical place where they sadly await the end of some theoretical age for their final judgment. When they met with physical death, chronological time ended for them. From their immortal perspective, the moment of their demise brought them face to face with the Judgment throne of God. At the Judgment their own unrepentant sinfulness condemned them to eternal separation from Holy God in a place of continuous suffering and unimaginable darkness prepared for Satan and the other fallen angels.

We know that the unrighteous have expired at different times and places since the beginning of time. What may be difficult to understand is that their resurrection to face the Judgment occurred simultaneously with the Judgment of all the unrighteous throughout history. To the rest of the world, they are dead and in their graves, but from their perspective, they all pass directly from this life into a Judgment Hall to meet God face to face.

For example, at the moment of Adolph Hitler's death, if he was unrepentant for his sins against God and humanity, he found himself at the Judgment. He was immediately standing not only with all of the Old Testament sinners, but also Attila the Hun, Genghis Khan, Al Capone, Jim Jones, and other notorious modern day sinners as well as billions of lesser known and unknown sinners. Included among the lesser known unrighteous are all people from every century who refused to acknowledge Jesus as their Savior and make him Lord of their lives. The Bible describes it as the great and small standing before the Lord for judgment (Revelation 20:12-15).

Although we tend to interpret the Judgment as a singular event that takes place at a definite time, we must confess that God's realm is timeless and His power is limitless. Though to us events take place in order of their occurrence, it must be understood that to a timeless God, all events occur simultaneously. He sees the past, present, and future all at once.

The human mind is not designed to comprehend the workings of the mind of God. His thoughts and His ability to think them are as high above our abilities as the heavens are above the earth (Isaiah 55:9). Yes, we are made in His likeness, but with finite limitations. God is infinite in all of His capabilities and characteristics. In the same way that His power is limitless, likewise His love is limitless. Due to His great mercy He has set His own limitations for the sake of mankind. His mercy endures forever (Psalms 106:1; 107:1; 118:1). We may only know things about God that He permits us to know. This is because our finite minds can not comprehend more about Him than He will allow for the present time. We can only know for sure that God is all that we can imagine and so much more than we are capable of imagining.

CHAPTER THIRTY

ISRAEL AFTER THE RAPTURE

In a recent series of sermons about the end times, a pastor friend of mine rendered his understanding about the role of Israel after the Rapture of the Church. Before proceeding, it must be understood that Israel is not the Church. Jews are without a doubt the chosen people of God with whom He has made an everlasting covenant (Genesis 17:7). However, their refusal to accept Jesus as their Messiah upon His first advent resulted in the loss of their holy temple and the loss of their status as a nation. Nonetheless, they remain the covenant people of God. Though they lost their national status in 70 AD and were dispersed throughout the world, God has major plans for them concerning the coming kingdom age. The fact that Israel became a nation again in 1948 provides a window into the important position they will occupy in these end times.

An exegesis of the parables found in the twenty-fourth chapter of Matthew can give us a post-rapture perspective concerning the nation of Israel. For instance, Jesus spoke of the separation of the sheep and goats in one parable. He said, "When you did it to the least of my brothers, you did it unto me." (Matthew 25:40) He was referring literally to His true brothers, the Jews. From this we see that Jesus is simply verifying the Word of God that visits God's blessings on those who bless Israel and His curses on those who curse Israel (Genesis 12:3). We understand that this is an eternal covenant that holds the rest of the world accountable for their treatment of Israel. This principle functioned even while they were living under God's pronouncement of dispersion.

For proof that God blesses those who support Israel we need go no farther than the United States. As a nation America has greatly respected and always aided Israel. Therefore, it is not surprising that the nations of the world who hate Israel also hate the United States! Currently, the battle cry of many Islamic nations calls for the annihilation of both Israel and the United States. People hate us because we support Israel! Certainly there can be no doubt that God has tremendously blessed the United States. Another reason for the out-pouring of blessings from above is undoubtedly linked to the evangelical outreach enterprises of Christians in America. Most of the people doing missionary work in the world come from the United States! Combining our evangelistic mission work with our support for Israel, it is easy to comprehend why God has blessed America.

When Jesus uses the illustration about the budding of the fig tree, we conclude that Israel's return to the holy land as a nation signified that budding (Mark 13:28-30). Israel is the fig tree. With its budding again as a nation in 1948, Jesus said that the time of His reappearing would be near. Notice that in Mark 11:13-14 Jesus approached a fig tree that had leaves but no fruit. He desired fruit, so He cursed the tree. Israel has again become a nation, but also rejects the Gospel which states that Jesus is the Messiah of God. As a result the people are without the Holy Spirit and are, therefore, incapable of bearing spiritual fruit. Those people will be cursed for not bearing fruit for God.

Another reference to Israel in Matthew 24 comes in the parable of the ten bridesmaids. The bride represents the Church of Jesus Christ, the bridegroom represents Jesus, and the bridesmaids represent Israel. According to Jewish tradition, the betrothal of the groom and bride is pre- arranged by their respective fathers. The marriage covenant is then signed by the groom and the bride. The two are espoused to be married at that point. This means they are legally married. However, they may not physically consummate the marriage until the groom has fulfilled his signed agreement to build a home for him and his bride. In Biblical times the home usually consisted of a room added onto the house of the groom's father. Completion of the home usually took one to two years. Only after the groom has prepared their abode is he permitted to come for his bride.

Let's pause here to point out some symbolism by which this custom likens itself to the return of the Lord. Believers in Jesus are the bride of Christ. Our marriage contract with Him was sealed by the receiving of the Holy Spirit. We are, therefore, sealed unto the day of His reappearing. Although we fellowship with the Lord through the Holy Spirit on a daily basis, we will not dwell with Him in person until He returns for us. Jesus told the disciples that He was going away to prepare an eternal dwelling place for them. He said that He would return for them so that they would forever be with Him in the place He had prepared (John 14:2-3)! He said that in His Father's house were many rooms. Paul wrote that Jesus would return like a thief in the night to take His bride away! He told us to watch for His return because we would not know the day or the hour when He will come (Matthew 24:36).

Another similarity between the ancient wedding customs and the reappearing of Jesus is seen at the Last Supper. After Jesus drank from the traditional cup of the Passover celebration, He told His disciples that He would not drink of the fruit of the vine again until He drank it with them in Heaven. A very similar statement is made at the ancient Jewish betrothal ceremony. The groom drinks the wine and states that he will not drink the wine again until he drinks it with his bride at the wedding feast. We are indeed the bride of Christ!

The ancient marriage customs of the Israelites would certainly be considered wild by Western standards! Resembling some comic opera, the groom is required to come like a thief in the night and abduct his bride. Under cover of night he takes her from her father's house to the place he has prepared. There the two will spend a seven-day honeymoon during which they must physically consummate their marriage. Of course, the bride has some vague idea concerning when the actual *abduction* will take place. When the time draws near, she selects her bridesmaids and makes ready for the coming event.

The bridesmaids play a significant role in the wedding abduction in that they keep watch with their lamps at night. The bridesmaids are awaiting the trumpet blast and the expectant call, "the bridegroom is coming!" After the call, the bridegroom sneaks into the back of the house of the bride and carries her off to their new abode. It is in every sense a staged elopement. The bridesmaids then follow the couple down the streets of the town in a festive processional to the new residence. When they reach their destination, the wedding party begins! After they retire, while the bride and groom are consummating their marriage, the wedding celebration party continues for up to seven days.

In the parable of Jesus (Matthew 25:1-13), we find that five of the ten bridesmaids do not have oil in their lamps. They have the lamps and they understand the purpose of the lamps, but they have not acquired the oil without which they cannot fulfill their purpose. Who are these unprepared bridesmaids? It has been suggested that they represent Jews during this era who are awaiting the coming of the groom but do not have what they need in order to participate in the celebration. The oil that they lack for their lamps is the Holy Spirit of God! Thus, they will not participate in the Rapture of the Church.

Let the reader understand that orthodox Jews are still awaiting the first coming of their Messiah! They know that He will come because His coming has been promised by God to their forefathers (Daniel 7:13-14). They do not believe that He has already come as Jesus, the Suffering Servant. They look for a High Commander and Deliverer who will arrive on a white stallion in the clouds and rule the nations from Jerusalem.

Throughout the Scriptures oil is used to symbolize the Holy Spirit. Therefore, in light of the parable of the bridesmaids we can declare that Jews who have not accepted Jesus as the Messiah, their Savior and Lord, do not possess the Holy Spirit, who is the seal of their redemption. When the Lord reappears for His Bride, the unrighteous, including Jews who are not believers, will not participate in the celebration we call the rapture. Every Jew who has accepted Jesus as Messiah will undoubtedly join the wedding feast because he or she possesses the Holy Spirit and is thus prepared for the reappearing of Jesus, the groom, at the rapture.

In the parable of the ten bridesmaids, it therefore seems right to summarize that the bride represents the Church, the bride-groom is the coming Lord Jesus, and the bridesmaids represent Israel. Some Jews have accepted Jesus as Messiah, Savior, and Lord. These are the bridesmaids that are allowed into the wedding feast. They have the oil (Holy Spirit) in their lamps. They can therefore light the way (evangelize) for the coming of the Bride-groom.

One may ask, "Why are converted Jews not considered the Bride in the previous interpretation?" All analogies fall apart at some point. It seems that in this interpretation the Bride represents the Gentiles that have been saved during the Age of Grace or the time of the Gentiles. The time for Israel's redemption is seen as yet to come. Jesus will indeed return to earth with His church after the seven years of post-rapture tribulation. The Jews will see the Messiah coming just as they have been promised. He will come in the clouds leading a mighty army (Daniel 7:13). He will be riding a white stallion. He will conquer the enemies of Israel, and He will then set up a thousand-year reign on earth. The seat of His global kingdom will be in Jerusalem. He will be the same Jesus that they rejected at His first advent!

In order to keep Israel under consideration as the bridesmaids, we must move from the rapture of the church to the second coming of Jesus. When Jesus comes in the clouds to rescue Israel, could the bridesmaids represent two types of Jews? Those Jews who believe that Jesus is their coming Messiah would be the Jews who are looking for Him to redeem Israel. The other camp would represent those Jews who are purely secular and cultural concerning their heritage and not in any way looking for the Messiah.

It must always be remembered that God cannot lie. That which He has promised to His chosen people will certainly come to pass. The deliverance they will receive will be far greater than what the first Century Jews were hoping for. Primarily they desired deliverance from Roman occupation and oppression. They also desired a place of prominence among the nations. Therefore, they could not accept the image of a suffering-servant type of Messiah. They did not see their need for deliverance from bondage to sin. After all, they had their religious system of sacrifices intact. Their sins were atoned for regularly and annually at high religious ceremonies. They were like many people of this century. The need for forgiveness from sin was the last thing they were concerned about. They wanted a King to provide them with economic advantage rather than a Savior who could repair their broken relationship with God.

Those who will be raptured will be those who have acknowledged both their sins and their need for a Savior. Upon such recognition they must believe the truth that Jesus is the one who has sacrificially paid the price for their sins. When people have believed that Jesus, as Messiah, has saved them from their sins, they must respond by making Him Lord of their lives. The response is marked by obedience to His commands and service to Him in carrying out His ongoing mission of global evangelism. All who reject Jesus as both God's sacrificial Lamb and the resurrected Lord have forfeited the eternal life that is reserved for those who not only accept these truths, but also live by them. Those who reject Jesus will participate in neither the rapture, nor the eternal bliss of the redeemed.

Israel is God's chosen people. They were chosen to provide a consecrated ancestry for the coming Messiah. Even so, what happened to the nation of Israel when they rejected the Messiah is a preview of what happens to all who reject the love of God in Jesus. Their suffering will be long and great. Every Jew who has died without Jesus as Savior will spend eternity in hell, as will every person of every nation who rejects the Son of God.

CHAPTER THIRTY-ONE

SIGNS OF THE TIMES

A. WARS AND RUMORS OF WAR

In the book of Matthew we find some very anxious disciples asking Jesus about His comments concerning the destruction of the temple (Matthew 24:3). Quite naturally they wanted to know some signs to look for. Like us today, they were intrigued as to what would become apparent before the end of the world as they knew it. More than two thousand years have come and gone since Jesus gave us God's answers to their questions. Is it any surprise that the world – even most of the Christians – must have stopped wondering about the signs that would occur prior to the reappearing of Jesus and the end of the Age of Grace?

Even during my lifetime (61 years) I have seen the world on the brink of self destruction several times! Today there are wars and rumors of wars to a much greater extent than at any other time since Jesus revealed His prophesy. Since the introduction and proliferation of nuclear weaponry among the nations, you must agree that at any moment the end of life as we know it is more likely than ever before. As a result of political instability and dictatorial rule in many third world countries, millions of people have been murdered. Many attempts at military occupation and government coups have resulted in genocidal activity. You could say that currently the value of human life is at an all-time low. You could also say that the love of many has waxed cold (Matthew 24:12)!

Recently someone published a list of the eight worst dictators of the current world scene. Interestingly, half of them were born around 1943. In the country of the number one worst dictator over 200,000 people were killed by the government in the past four years. Under this dictator's leadership 5.3 million people have been driven from their homes and more than 700,000 have fled the country.

The number two worst dictator has shut off his people from the world while building up an impressive army and becoming a potential nuclear threat. Another of the worst dictators has violated human rights in twenty-two areas of concern. Among those concerns listed by the U. S. State Department are torture, forced abortion, detention of religious groups, restrictions on speech and the media, and public execution for non-violent crimes.

In one of the countries ruled by a dictator the health and welfare of his constituents has suffered tremendously. The average life-span is thirty-seven years for men and thirty-four years for women. That country also has a twenty-five percent orphan rate and an annual inflation rate of 1,281%.

The dictators mentioned in previous paragraphs join a long list of pagan dictators who have wreaked havoc during recent world history. Who can forget the anti-Semitic regime of Adolph Hitler that led to the genocide of an estimated six million Jews? Add to that the dictators that fanned the flames of World Wars during the Twentieth Century. Millions were killed during wartime and many more millions were adversely affected in the aftermath following the wars.

There is no doubt that this generation, despite all of its sophisticated and technological peace-keeping weaponry is farther from world peace than ever before. This surely is a sign of the times that Jesus spoke of. The answer to man's inability to control his own hunger for power is not to be found in a League of Nations or the United Nations. A closer look reveals that the countries forming such organizations are neither in league with one another, nor are they united in the cause of world peace. The plain truth is that the world, under the guise of preparing for more peaceful times, is actually placing in the grasp of tyrannical, power-hungry men the means that God will use to scorch the current earth once and for all. It is all part of God's plan!

B. PESTILENCE & DISASTERS

Jesus also referred to world-wide plagues as a sign of the end (Matthew 24:7). Although the world of the Twenty-first Century now possesses some of the most brilliant, scientific minds in its history, the spread of incurable diseases continues to ravage its population. The incurable disease of

AIDS respects neither age, nor race, nor gender, nor social status. Even though hunger is not a disease as such, people around the globe face disaster as they are starving to death by the millions.

A missionary in Kenya told me that 25% of the population was under fifteen years old. Of that segment of the population, half were orphaned either because of the death of their parents or abandonment. The main contributor to the problem has been identified as unrestrained sexual activity out of wedlock. This activity not only results in population explosion, but in the seemingly uncontrolled spread of sexually-transmitted diseases. Syphilis and gonorrhea are at epidemic levels. These diseases account for a 50% death-at-birth rate.

Another problem on the rise is both the ineptitude and the corruption of local governments in foreign countries concerning distribution of donated food supplies. Much of the food rots before distribution. Some of the food is secretly sold to other countries. Along with serious drought conditions, the lack of food supply has brought about increased malnutrition problems as well as economic disaster.

Lack of proper nutrition gives rise to the body's susceptibility to disease. Is the death of millions of innocent children each year due to starvation or to the diseases brought on by famine? Is the problem horrible dictatorial leadership, or is it the inability of other, more fortunate nations to see and properly respond to the plight of the innocent? Comparatively speaking however, an even greater plague is taking place in modern America.

C. JUST LIKE THE DAYS OF NOAH

We can easily agree that since the dawn of the Twentieth Century millions of people around the world have died due to World Wars, political unrest, famines and plagues. We could also argue whether or not any of those deaths could have been prevented and by what means. America is the greatest nation on the planet in terms of scientific, economic, and spiritual advancement. And yet millions of innocent pre-borns have been systematically and legally murdered over the past thirty-six years.

Our constitution holds that this nation will be governed by its people. Therefore, these heinous acts of murder for the sake of social convenience are not only permitted *by* the American people, they are actually *funded* by us! No doubt some liberal constitutionalist will defensively jump up and say that it was the Supreme Court composed of *non-elected* Justices that made abortion-on-demand the rule of law in America. Isn't anyone concerned that it was God Almighty who made the ruling, *Thou Shalt Not Kill?* Incidentally, even though the Supreme Court may make a ruling concerning what is constitutionally legitimate, that ruling must be written up as a law and voted on by Congress. It then must be signed into law by a sitting President. Our Congressmen and the President are elected by us! Therefore, we're the guilty party who has endorsed legalized abortion!

The meaning of *Thou Shalt Not Kill* is empirically clear. The Lord's Commandment was referencing the murder of the innocent. Who in any society is more innocent than a child in the womb? Of course, by now Americans are completely desensitized to both *that* rule and any other rule of God. This is mostly due to the satanic influence of those who shriek the words *separation of church and state* every time God's laws are introduced into a political arena. When Jesus comes for His Church, there will definitely be a sudden and irrevocable *separation of Church and state!*

Jesus said that the time of His reappearing would be like the days of Noah. In the midst of the legislated immorality in America the question must be asked: When Jesus appears as the Ark of rescue from the destruction that will follow, will you be standing on the side of the Church or the State? Let's ponder another statement made by Jesus. Render unto Caesar, in this case *the State*, that which is Caesar's; and unto God, the ultimate authority, that which is God's. The context of this statement obviously calls for those who know the heart of Jesus to defer to God's rule in any and all areas of conflicting sovereignty.

We have two strong Biblical references with which to evaluate the current status quo in America and the world. Let's reconsider the first destruction of nearly all life on the planet... God's flood! We know that God made His purposes known to Moses, who then wrote the account of God's reasons for the flood (Genesis 6:5-7). The picture of man's wickedness that we have from the Genesis account is not a great deal unlike the moral disintegration of the world today. I will restrict my editorial comparison to the nation with whose history I am most familiar.

The United States was formed by God-fearing men, many of whom were Christians. The ideals that sustain our form of government were Biblical in nature. They unquestionably embraced godly, moral decency within our developing American culture. Life, liberty, and the pursuit of happiness were, in the mindset of those colonial God-fearers, necessary to the formation of a godly and, subsequently, God-blessed society. Godly, in this context, refers to morality that is based on the Biblical model. Such morality includes sexual purity, personal piety, and respect for the laws and statutes of Almighty God. I should also mention that our moral nation, as a godly respecter of others, has not attempted to conquer the rest of the nations! Instead, our posture has been defensive as opposed to offensive. We have nurtured and assisted rather than conquered other nations.

One must either be too young or must possess a complete lack of understanding to miss the fact that God has indeed blessed America! In a relatively short amount of time this nation has risen to world prominence on the shoulders of the godly men who desired to form a godly nation for the glory of their God. Their writings are filled with the language of dependence upon God for not only their immediate success, but for the success of future generations of Americans. An atheist looks at the design of the world and fosters a belief in the big bang theory. Likewise, only an atheist could track the history of the struggle for American independence and believe it all *just happened* apart from divine intervention!

America has not only sent out more Christian missionaries to more places around the world, but has also given more money to more needy countries than any other sovereign nation. It is unquestionable that as long as America remains a nation under God's leadership she will be blessed by God!

However, because the Scripture teaches that the nation whose God is the Lord will receive His blessing, the end of God's blessings on America must surely be at hand. It can be summed up in the phrase *separation of church and state*, which is more correctly worded *the separation of God from American political policy.* I hope the reader knows that anything separated from God is doomed to self-destruction!

D. LIKE SODOM AND GOMORRAH

A phrase that I have already referred to among conservative evangelist camps goes like this, "If God does not judge America, He owes Sodom and Gomorrah an apology!" Not only can we glimpse a picture of America's potential future judgment from the account of the great flood, but what about the current rise of unbridled homosexuality? To think for a moment that God has changed His vast and unmovable mind concerning the gross sin of homosexuality is to state one's ignorance as to His unchanging holiness and His full dominion!

Hollywood leftists will no doubt jump up and shriek, "Mean spirited, bigoted, Moral Right Wing Conservative!" These and many other politically correct terms are commonly associated with those who say that homosexuality is morally and Biblically wrong! The moment they mutter such nonsense is the moment they have *outted* themselves as ignorant pagans.

Do they really not know that it is God who has warned all nations against the sin of homosexuality as an abomination? He warned us through the example of Sodom and Gomorrah. In that scenario the homosexuals were so abased that they would even have raped God's angelic messengers! In His mercy God had agreed with Abraham that if His messengers could find at least ten righteous people in Sodom, He would spare the whole population (Genesis 18:32). Well, they couldn't, and so God didn't!

God's obvious answer for those who embrace homosexuality could not be clearer. The real wake-up sign for the rest of this nation is seen in the total and infernal destruction of Sodom and Gomorrah. It can be supposed that not all of the residents of the cities were homosexuals. It must be inferred, however, that because the whole population *embraced* the homosexual lifestyle, they were considered immoral by the Lord God. Only immoral people embrace immorality! Does the American majority embrace homosexuality as a normal lifestyle? Do you?

At this writing five states have superior court rulings on the books that sanction and permit marriage of same-sex partners. There is reason to suspect that by the time you have read these words *that* number could have doubled or quadrupled! Indeed, the end of all morality in America is rapidly approaching. What kind of place will this country be for our children or grandchildren? This kind of warning from the Word of God should cause us to step up our efforts in evangelizing our communities before it is too late. It is certain that a post-rapture world will be pro-homosexual.

Do those who claim to be sexually attracted to members of their same sex not know the truth about their desires? They have been deceived by Satan into adopting an unnatural lust for people of their own gender (Romans 1:24-32). Homosexuality is part of Satan's evil plan to pervert and confuse individuals concerning God's loving plan for their lives. The perfect plan of God for most individuals includes marriage between a man and a woman. This is the Biblically correct model for an ordered and godly society. Some individuals, for moral and spiritual reasons only, may choose not to marry. For everyone else the standing order from God still applies – we are to populate His earth. That kind of proliferation occurs only within the Biblically accepted concept of marriage between a man and a woman. Please tell me. How do Homosexuals procreate? On second thought please don't!

Those who have read the Scripture or who have been informed as to God's position on homosexuality must make an important choice. Suppose a man finds himself sexually stimulated by the outward appearance of another man. The choices are twofold. He can obey God's Word which, for his own good, instructs him to flee the appearance of evil and to avoid temptation. Or, he can choose to serve the interests of his own fleshly desires, call God a liar, and pursue hell at full speed.

How can a man or woman of the age of consent keep themselves pure in the sight of God when they claim to have sexual desires for members of their same sex? I suggest that someone must seek one of several answers rather than to disobey God's commands. The first step is always upward.

One must ask God with all sincerity why such feelings are emerging. The answer is always going to be that all feelings leading us away from God are designed by Satan to lead us toward our own destruction. Therefore, individuals must realize that Satan is tempting them through unnatural and unholy leanings in order to separate them not only from God, but from the wonderful purpose that God has designed for them.

"But," some may say, "I get a sick feeling inside when I think about sex with someone of the opposite sex!" Think about such a statement in light of what God has said is normal for men and women. If it is normal, but you feel sick about it, something is wrong with both your understanding of God's plan and your appreciation of the opposite gender. Obviously, most young boys and girls get a 'yucky' feeling when they are forced to think about intimacy with the opposite gender.

Possibly you have been misled during your formative years as to the appropriate relationship between a man and a woman. You may have been deprived of the role model of one or both loving parents. Maybe you never witnessed the tenderness of a man toward his wife and vice versa. The worst-case scenario is that you were sexually abused as a young child and, therefore, possess unresolved sexual frustration concerning the opposite sex.

Perhaps you grew up without restraints regarding your internet surfing. You may have fallen prey to the huge numbers of porn sites that are growing on a daily basis. This pertains to sex acts between members of the opposite sex. Someone will no doubt ask how constantly viewing *straight* porn can pervert the mind of a child. Only someone who is already perverted would ask such a question! A Christian watching others commit adultery, pedophilia, incest, and fornication is forcing the Holy Spirit to take part in such acts. For non-believers, it is the same as being involved in such activities. Jesus said that if a man looks upon a woman with lust, he has committed adultery with her in his heart.

The obvious question is, "How is a person viewing sexual activity between members of the opposite sex drawn toward homosexuality?" The answer is clinical. There is the risk of desensitization toward normal sexual activities. The Apostle Paul wrote that men and women were so desperately involved with sexual immorality that God gave them over to the pursuit of un-natural sexual acts (Romans 1:24-32). As a result of unrestricted sexual exploration individuals can find themselves addicted to completely perverted pornographic behaviors.

The Bible states that when we adopt an immoral lifestyle, God gives us over to a base mind. Such people become so perverse in their thinking about sex that literally *anything goes!* They eventually become sexually aroused even by members of the same sex. The bottom of the barrel finds them involved in bestiality! A constant diet of pornographic material creates a sex-fiend mentality. The Bible says that as a man thinks, so he is! There is no way to escape God's universal reality that a man becomes whatever fills his mind.

The principal crime one commits concerning homosexuality is that of agreeing it is not offensive to God and, therefore is also not offensive to civilization in general. God says that homosexuality leads to the downfall of any society that embraces it. Failure to heed God's warning always leads to self destruction. Those who desire a healthy society need only obey God's Word. Homosexuality cannot be tolerated in a godly society. It is more than an abomination to God; it is the formula for self destruction for any nation.

As America has unwittingly embraced the homosexual lifestyle there has been a greater reporting of pedophilia than ever before. Think about it. Today homosexuals are free to enlist young children into their cultic society during this era of increased immorality. God has made it clear that all sexual relationships outside of marriage are also outside His moral design for mankind and an ordered society. This means that fornication for the unwed and adultery for married couples are mentally, emotionally, and physically detrimental to the individual and to human society as well.

E. THE MEDIA-SHAPED CULTURE

The decay of morality in America has increased exponentially with each passing decade since the 1950s. If you watched America's favorite married couple of the '50s on television, you saw Desi Arnaz and Lucille Ball sleeping in separate beds with pajamas buttoned up to the neck! Think about it. The couple was actually married in real life! However, the moral codes of '50s TV shows would not permit viewers to see a couple in the same bed!

Imagine how many of today's TV shows would be banned by the broadcast gatekeepers of 1950! Today there are very few moral standards for TV programming. In fact, the more sexual connotations and innuendos, the more likely the shows will be financially successful! May God forgive the Christians who sat silently and watched the rapid deterioration of moral programming standards! As movies and television sank deeper into the sinful mire of heterosexually explicit themes, another abomination began to be firmly seated as a favorite media theme.

The movies were the first mainstream media to introduce homosexual themes. The homosexual lifestyle was generally used for comic relief at first. However, the growing homosexual culture in California began to demand serious treatment in the name of equality. They felt their social plight simply had to receive national attention. Subsequently, in recent decades there has been an increase in displays of homosexual relationships on nearly all prime time sit-com programming. You might say they were out of their closets and into our living rooms! The question is, how did the homosexual movement gain favor over such a relatively short period of time? Did gay rights activists wave their banner high enough to gain recognition in the courts as a persecuted minority? Enter the once morally-centered United States government and the non-elected Judicial Branch.

I have purposely separated the U. S. Government from the Judicial Branch for an important reason. The Supreme Court is supposed to judge court cases as to their constitutionality. However, the court has on many occasions ruled against both the constitutional ideals and the will of the majority of Americans. America was founded upon constitutional law and sustained by democratic rule by the majority vote of the electorate. However, Supreme Court justices are not elected by the people. They are appointed by the President and confirmed by the Congress for life. Therefore, they are permitted to execute a power of legislation based on the majority decisions between nine non-elected people. How else do you think the homosexual agenda has been able to transform itself from a twisted, Biblically-abominable lifestyle to a silly, laughable lifestyle and finally to a constitutionally protected minority status?

If you are under thirty years of age and are also Biblically illiterate, you haven't noticed this cultural metamorphosis. For that reason you probably would join the growing number of desensitized young Americans in calling the previous paragraph *mean spirited*! That's okay! In this generation much of the truth is generally labeled as mean spirited. Believers need not be so outraged! All of this behavior was described by Jesus. We have always known that this generation was coming. It is actually very exciting to see the fulfillment of end-time prophesies, as awful as these signs are!

Perhaps the greatest disappointment that I have encountered is the treatment of the name of Jesus. The name of Jesus was and is and shall be, until the day of His reappearing, the only name under heaven given among men whereby we must be saved! After His reappearing at the Rapture of the Church, Gentiles will not be able to receive salvation through His name until the coming of His kingdom on earth! After the rapture, Jews who are looking for Messiah will be saved by the return of the Lord Jesus. When Jesus said that there was no way to the Father except through Him, He meant His name!

In an article in a Christian Music magazine a member of a very successful Christian band said, "It's hard to use the name of Jesus in a song without sounding *cheesy*." In 2007, at a meeting with one of the most successful Christian Radio Promoters in Nashville, I was told, "The name of Jesus is too much of an affront to many of the listeners in the marketing area of the more successful Christian Radio stations. So I choose to promote the songs where the pronouns are used rather than the actual name of Jesus." The same week of that meeting I researched the top ten Contemporary Christian songs on the Billboard Survey. There was no mention of the name of Jesus in the top twelve Christian songs. The name of Jesus was used only five times in the top twenty-five songs!

What does it say to you when the Christian songs in an era do not mention the name of Jesus? Sounds to me like the end is very, very near!

CHAPTER THIRTY-TWO

CONCLUSIONS

Based on the eye-witness reports of His disciples concerning the teachings of Jesus, we know that He will return to the earth in order to take His church to heaven to be with Him (John 14:2-3). Many agree with the return of Jesus, but believe that He will only return for His millennial rule over the earth. These do not believe in a literal snatching-away or rapture. In fact, there are nearly as many different teachings about the rapture as there are different denominations. Concerning the millennium, many believe that John the revelator saw the end of the thousand years in his revelation (Revelation 21:1-3). He said that heaven and earth had passed away, and that New Jerusalem came down from the clouds adorned as a bride. He spoke of a new eternal earth with New Jerusalem as the capital. He said that God would be with His people. God will provide light and life for all in that new realm.

There is no way that every possible belief concerning the rapture, the millennium, and eternity can be treated by just one book without containing several volumes. Suffice it to say that after Jesus returns with His church, and after His millennial reign, heaven and earth will be replaced by a new eternal existence to be enjoyed by Him and those who have believed in Him. This writer believes that Scripture indicates a reappearing of Jesus, at which time He will rapture His church to be with Him forever. He will rapture all the resurrected believers and all the believers who are alive at the time of His reappearing. He will then, following a seven-year tribulation period on earth, bring His raptured church with Him to reign over the earth for a thousand years. To dispute what will happen afterwards would be an exercise unworthy of His true disciples. I believe the whole truth would be too much for us in our present finite state of mind.

Also, we know by His words to His disciples that no man can know the day or the hour of His reappearing. The great Missionary-Apostle Paul wrote that for those who do not know Him, it will occur like a thief in the night – it will be completely unexpected! However, Jesus gave to His followers several definite signs that will precede His reappearing. The varied chronology of the signs makes the exact time impossible for anyone to figure out. Just like the bride in ancient Jewish tradition, we will have a pretty good idea when the time is near. He gave us many clues designed to alert His church as to the approaching season of our rapture. He also instructed His followers in every age to do three primary things: to obey His commandments, to evangelize and make disciples, and to watch and pray.

When Jesus raptures His church, the resurrected bodies of the dead in Christ will be changed and will rise into the air. The bodies of the faithful believers who are alive at the rapture will also be instantly changed so that they can exist in the eternal realm of heaven. They will then rise to meet with the Lord and the others. Jesus said that the physical rapture of living believers will be observable by the rest of the population. Beware of anyone who says that many Gentiles who rejected Christ would then see that He is real and believe in Him for salvation! Oh, they'll believe alright! Just like the demons believe and tremble! The problem for them will be that the Age of Grace will have closed. The Gentiles left behind will then believe anything other than the fact that they have missed salvation!

Paul wrote that the Holy Spirit, who is the agent of salvation, will be taken out of the earth realm with the raptured believers (2 Thessalonians 2:7). This will usher in a seven-year era of tribulation on the earth. Due to the absence of the Holy Spirit, there will be no restraining force to keep the man of lawlessness, the Antichrist, in check. The world will quickly revert to its pre-flood state characterized by total corruption and perversion (except for Noah and his family). This time the remnant of people faithful to God will be those Jews who are still looking for the coming of the Messiah.

Many who at present only perceive of themselves as Christians but resist the Lordship of Jesus and the rule of the Holy Spirit will not take part in the rapture. In several of His parables Jesus indicated that there are many who will not participate in the kingdom because of their selfishness, greed, slothfulness, and general unpreparedness. The Apostle Paul, inspired by the Holy Spirit, posted several lists containing the lifestyle actions that will keep people from participating in the kingdom of God. The Apostle John reiterated this list in the book of Revelation. Others will actually argue with the Lord as to their worthiness of inheriting eternal life based on their good works (Matthew 25:44). With the glut of cults and false religions that have appeared in recent decades, many will miss heaven due to sheer ignorance of the Word of God.

Just imagine what kind of impact the church of Jesus Christ could have had on the nations had it not been for inter-denominationalism. The very idea of dividing the body of Christ into various specialized groups, each with their own peculiar doctrines, flies in the face of the unity called for in the Word of God. Unity is the strength of the church. To suggest other-wise is to follow Satan's master plan to divide and conquer! The idea of a different church on every corner is foreign to the master plan of the Savior, who taught the concept of unifica-tion through global evangelization. Jesus said that a house divided against itself cannot stand (Matthew 12:25).

Denominationalism is a tool of Satan for the weakening of the evangelism arm of the church of Jesus Christ. This being true, it is not difficult to see that many whole denominations are in jeopardy. By subscribing to a doctrine arrived at by disagree-ment or misinterpretation of Scripture, several church groups have overlooked the call of God to unite for the purpose of global evangelization. As a result the simple message of the love of God for all people has become multi-faceted and diver-sified so as to render it complex, mystifying, and unattainable by many. The weightiness of multiple creeds and doctrines has only served to camouflage the basic ideal. In many cases a person would need a master's degree and years of heavy indoctrination before attaining the understanding necessary to become a full-fledged member of some denominations! Jesus said that unless people become as children, they cannot enter into the kingdom of God (Matthew 18:3).

After the church is raptured, the opportunity for salvation will be over for Gentiles for seven years. The Age of Grace will have come to an end. An era of judgment for the non-Jewish pagan nations will begin. After the rapture, America will be one of those pagan nations. No doubt many church services will continue. However, regardless of how many theologians avow that a Gentile can still be saved after the rapture, it is simply not possible. Because of the absence of the Holy Spirit in this realm, it is not even arguable that some may have a second chance at salvation. The presence of the Holy Spirit is necessary for salvation.

How then will people be saved? If they should say that they believe in Jesus because they have *observed* the physical disappearance of the church, where is their faith? *Seeing* does not enable people to believe in Jesus. Rather, it is the faith-act of *believing* that enables people to see God's kingdom! One might say that belief in Jesus is not an *eye* thing, but a *heart* thing. The Gospel message is applied to your heart by the Holy Spirit and you believe! If you have to see Jesus or the effects of His Gospel to believe in Him, you'll neither see Him nor the effects of His Gospel.

Imagine a group of people who suddenly are aware that thousands of Christians have disappeared from the face of the earth. If they had considered themselves to be Christian, their reaction will most likely be one of great regret. Many will realize that Jesus has taken the true believers out of this world. They will instantly understand that they were not among the true believers, and that they have been left behind with the rest of the unbelieving world. They will be very sad and emotionally traumatized. Weep, wail, repent, and pray as they may, the time for Gentiles to accept Jesus as Savior and Lord will have passed. Their ultimate conclusion must be that they rejected the Gospel that was presented to them, and they must face the potential of the eternal punishment they have chosen.

Even some of the world's most renowned and beloved philanthropists, psychologists, moralists and socialists will miss the rapture. The reason is childlike in nature. Regardless of the stature one attains according to the world's value system, there is only one way to gain eternal life. Jesus said that He is the only way to the Father. Unless a man is born again, he cannot enter the kingdom of God. Being a seeker of the kingdom is important, but coming to the point of personally accepting the saving grace that you find is what makes the eternal difference. The great men who reject the Gospel of Jesus Christ will not inherit the kingdom of God. Nor will those who are more concerned with the physical needs of people than with their spiritual needs. Nor will the church members who insist that people know where their church is, and they can come if they've a mind to!

After the rapture, many church members will exist in a state of denial. They, like the rest of the world, will be susceptible to any reasonable explanation as to the disappearance of people who just happened to be members of Christian churches. Without the guidance and the convicting influence of the Holy Spirit, they will adapt quickly to whatever conspiracy theory the press hands down. When the chaotic results of such a massive and mysterious departure subside, people will return to business as usual.

Because of the chaos caused by the rapture, the stage will be set for a strangely empowered individual to rise to power. Many will be seeking explanations for the disappearance of so many people. The general population will be primed to hear from a supernaturally endowed, charismatic person, who will be standing by with logical explanations. This Antichrist will feed the people what they will need to hear in order to line up with his one-world-order mentality. Because of the absence of the Holy Spirit, such a charismatic person will have no trouble deceiving the nations into believing that they need to follow him (2 Thessalonians 2:9-12). He will set himself up as the ruler of the world, and will eventually describe himself as God (2 Thessalonians 2:4).

Following the rapture there will be seven years during which the Antichrist will rise to world domination. In order to gain the allegiance of the people of the earth he will perform supernatural signs and wonders. His powers will come from Satan. The absence of the Holy Spirit as a restraining force will enable him to command the respect of nearly everyone in the world. His powers will be so convincing that even believers, had they not been raptured, might have been deceived. He will bring the world together under a one-world government with him as the totalitarian dictator. Everyone under his rule will be connected to the government for their very existence.

Three and a half years into the rule of the Antichrist, He will announce to the great satisfaction of most of the world that he is none other than God Almighty. At this point the Jews who still consider themselves the covenant people of God will disavow their loyalty and break their alliance with him. He will rally the other nations against Israel, thus beginning the countdown to the end of this world at Armageddon. Following three years of threats and sanctions, the Antichrist will prepare the nations for the final assault against the tiny nation of Israel.

An army of Biblical proportions from the East and North will march against God's people in a final attempt to obliterate their last hope concerning God's promise of ultimate salvation. At this point, seven years after the rapture, Jesus will return to the earth. Whereas, the first time He came as a frail and helpless infant, this time He will come as a mighty, avenging conqueror. The first time He came to deliver Israel and the whole world from sin. This time He will come to deliver Israel from the hands of a world of sinners. The first time He came as an Israelite to establish peace in the hearts of men. This time He will come to the Israelites to establish a kingdom on earth. The first time He spoke not a word in His own defense. This time He will destroy the advancing armies of the enemies of God with a single word. The Word of God will come as the King of kings and the Lord of lords to rule for a thousand years as the Prince of Peace!

CHAPTER THIRTY-THREE

I AM A PRE-TRIBBER — REVELATION 19

The following is an explanation of Revelation 19:
The scene takes place in heaven with people praising the Lord (vs. 1). This is the Apostle John's vision. The context is concerning events that are taking place in heaven leading up to the Second Coming of Jesus to the earth. Notice that those who are praising Jesus are not just angelic beings, but people — the raptured redeemed!

In verse 2 the people in heaven continue to praise Jesus for His righteous judgment of the great whore. Many theologians believe this to be the Roman Catholic Church whose 'smoky' punishment will go on forever (vs. 3). One may ask how such judgment could come on a "Christian" organization. Here's a picture for you: Imagine a multimillion dollar cathedral, complete with costly and highly ornate trappings including statues of various *saints* and the *Virgin Mary*. Imagine clergymen in highly ostentatious and extremely expensive attire, including bejeweled headdresses and scepters. Imagine the pretentious, pompous processionals when these individuals parade through their elaborate realm as smoke is wafted before and behind them. Now think about the source of the money to put on such ceremonies. Look outside the cathedral and see some of the world's poorest people struggling to eke out a living in the shadow of the monstrous edifice that their tithes support.

Verses 4-6 feature continued praise and worship of Jesus. Now the praise is demanded of all who are in heaven.

Verses 7-9 describe the marriage of the Lamb and the great wedding feast. Those who have made themselves ready through preparation are now considered the wife. The wife has arrayed herself in fine linen that is pure and bright. The fine linen symbolizes the righteous acts of the redeemed that are blessed to participate in the marriage supper of the Lamb.

In verse 10, seeing the Church wedded to her Savior and Lord, John is overwhelmed with awe to the point of bowing before the messenger. John is told not to worship fellow servants, but God alone.

Verses 11-16 show Jesus with His army coming to earth for the final battle. Jesus is called by several of His prophesied names including; The Word of God, King of kings, and Lord of lords. His accompanying army is also on white horses and wearing their fine linen that is pure and white.

In verses 17 & 18 an angel calls all the birds of the air to prepare to feast on the remains of the bodies of the wicked slain in the battle. Notice that the slain include Kings, Captains, mighty men, horses and riders and ALL other men. This proves that there will be no believers on the earth when

Jesus returns. It also reveals the truth concerning His rhetorical question, "Will the Son of Man find faith on the earth when He returns?"

Verses 19-21 show the wicked army coming against the Lord and His army. The Beast and the False Prophet are defeated and thrown into the lake of fire. All the others are killed by the Sword of Jesus. The sword is the word from His mouth. The birds finish off the remains of those slain.

Thanks to the grace and mercy of the Lord Jesus, I will be one of the redeemed *with* Him at the feast. And the feast will occur prior to Him and all the other redeemed of the Lord coming to save Israel at the Battle of Armageddon. There may be other translations of these verses and other methods of shifting the order of the occurrence of these events, but the Holy Spirit testifies to my spirit that this is the truth. I am not afraid to face whatever persecution Satan wishes to throw at me. However, I thank the Lord for His enduring mercy toward those He has redeemed from the suffering intended for those who have rejected Him during the Age of Grace known as the time of the Gentiles. That time ends with the Rapture of the Church.

The Bible states that Jesus will return to earth in the clouds, and that His church will be with Him. His church will be with Him when He returns because *He will have previously raptured those who believe in Him!* His return will be timely concerning the nation of Israel. When it appears that embattled Israel is about to be completely annihilated, Jesus will return and instantly defeat all of its enemies with a single word. Vastly superior to any other power in existence, the returning

Christ will display for all of mankind the incomparable distinction between the Creator and that which He has created. In a magnificent manifestation of both mercy and might He will destroy the Antichrist and chain Satan in a pit for a thousand years. He will then begin His millennial reign of peace over all the earth.

The Church that will return to the earth with Jesus will consist of those who have been raptured at the end of the Age of Grace. Jesus said that His followers would judge angels and nations. Does this mean that during the millennial reign of Christ on earth believers with their new supernatural bodies will rule as a super race of governing peacekeepers? Will they shape a new righteous frontier during the thousand years of Satan's exile? Will they, as super evangelists, finally complete the Lord's on-going, ultimate mission of global evangelism? Whereas the answers to all of these questions have been hinted at in the Scriptures, it is not for us to know the times or epochs that are limited to God's foreknowledge (Acts 1:7).

One purpose of this book has been to point out what will happen to believers and non-believers when Jesus accomplishes the Rapture of the Church. Though scripturally based, some of the suggestions as to what will occur after the rapture have been purely conjectural on the part of this author. I claim no special revelation from the Lord Jesus other than that which He has already revealed in His Word. The primary purpose of this book is to refute the lie that has been told regarding Gentiles who have rejected Jesus before the rapture. It is my belief that they cannot receive another chance to accept Him after the rapture and during the seven years of the Tribulation.

A hopeful result of this book is that believers will quickly begin whatever preparation they deem necessary in their personal lives in order to be ready for the reappearing of Jesus. Do you have unregenerate friends or loved ones? Do you believe that you can avoid sharing the Gospel with them now in favor of leaving behind a video tape or DVD to explain how salvation can be obtained after the rapture? Though perceived as an offering of mercy and grace, such a perspective must be viewed as the ultimate deception. To put off showing the way of salvation to someone that you know to be lost is to point out how mediocre and unimportant you believe your own salvation to be.

God's Word tells us that today is the day of salvation! There can be no greater sense of urgency and immediacy placed on the importance of preaching Jesus as Savior and Lord than this! The scriptural warning means there are no guarantees that any lost person will ever see tomorrow. Let the reader who has not responded to the love of God in Jesus be advised and encouraged to receive His salvation from sin today while the Age of Grace is in full bloom.

In spite of what some misguided or false prophets have promised, there will be no second chance for lost Gentiles. God desires that none perish. God offers you both the forgiveness of sin and eternal life in heaven with Him. He sent His Son, Jesus, to die for your sins. Only the blood of the Son of God has the power to cleanse you of all unrighteousness and bring about your adoption into the eternal family of God. You can receive all the blessings of God, including the presence of His Holy Spirit to guide you into all truth. To as many as believe in Jesus, God gives the power to be called His sons!

My prayer for believers is that this book has created a sense of godly urgency regarding the end of the Age of Grace. I urge you to redouble your efforts to share the Gospel with as many people as you can, because you do not know the day or the hour of the reappearing of the Lord. Please recommit yourself to maintain a lifestyle of evangelism. May you be known as the person who is always talking about Jesus! Let your light so shine before men that they, seeing your good works, will glorify your Father which is in heaven. Strive to be more like the light of the world that Jesus said His believers must be!

Dear brothers and sisters in Christ, bear the torch of Christianity to as many people as you can and in such a way that you will be able to give the same testimony as Paul the Apostle who said, "I have fought the good fight...I have run the race!" We must live in such a way that we will be able to say as John the Revelator said,

"Even so, come Lord Jesus!"

Printed in the USA
CPSIA information can be obtained
at www.ICGtesting.com
CBHW031422220724
11946CB00027B/168

9 781615 797882